REALWRITE

realtime ©

Computerized Shorthand Writing System

DRILL BOOK

SECOND EDITION

ROBERT W. MCCORMICK
CAROLEE FREER

PEARSON

Prentice
Hall

ISBN 0-13-118053-3

This book is dedicated to the court reporting students at
Alfred State College, Alfred, NY and
Cypress College, Cypress, CA
who were the forerunners
in developing and
perfecting the
theory.

TABLE OF CONTENTS

PHRASE DRILLS

INTRODUCTION

Lesson Drills

This *DrillBook* is meant to accompany the *Realwrite/realtime LessonBook*. This book contains 24 drills, one for every two lessons found in the *LessonBook*. In addition, there is an exercise found in the *NoteBook* to be used with each unit.

The drills are divided into various exercises, which include such things as drills on words, short forms, phrases, names, numbers, vocabulary, and so on. The final section of each drill contains a practical exercise which will allow you to practice everything that was taught in the corresponding lessons.

It is important that you practice each word, short form, phrase, and practical exercise until you can write them without hesitation.

This *DrillBook* is meant to supplement and complement the theory that you will learn in the *LessonBook* and to give you practical experience in writing *Realwrite*. The *NoteBook* should be used to give you practice in reading and transcribing *Realwrite* notes.

Phrase Drills

The second part of the *DrillBook* is made up of a series of "phrase drills" which will emphasize some of the basic phrases that you learned. In addition, some advanced phrases will be introduced for you to learn and practice.

One of the key ingredients to gaining initial speed is through the use of short forms and phrases. It is important for you to learn your shortcuts (short forms and phrases) so that you can write them and read them back quickly and without any hesitation.

Begin Now

Follow the instruction given in your *LessonBook*. They will tell you when to do each drill and exercises found in the *DrillBook* and *NoteBook*.

UNIT 1
DRILL I (Lessons 1-2)

General Information

It is important for you to learn from the beginning that the realtime writer is concerned with WORDS--words are your business.

You should develop a habit of appreciating WORDS in their various forms. You should write down new words that you hear and look up their meanings. You should make a conscientious effort to develop your vocabulary by learning and using a new word every day.

In studying words it is important to realize that a word is a series of sounds that are vocalized, and sounds are a series of consonants and/or vowels.

A consonant is a sound that is produced by a combination of the mouth, tongue, and lips. The consonants are:

B C D F G H J K L M N P Q R S T V W X Y Z

Some consonants can be "hard" or "soft." A hard "C" sounds like "K" while a soft "C" sounds like an S.

A vowel is a sound that is produced by the passage of air through the windpipe and exiting the mouth. The vowels are:

A E I O U and sometimes Y

A vowel can be "long" or "short." A long vowel generally sounds like the vowel itself. Generally speaking:

The long "A" sounds like the "a" in "place."
The long "E" sounds like the "e" in "street."
The long "I" sounds like the "i" in "right."
The long "O" sounds like the "o" in "poke."
The long "U" may sound like the "u" in "pure."

Words can also be divided into syllables. A syllable is the number of consonant/vowel combinations that make up a word. Some words contain only one syllable (Joan) while others may contain two (Joann) or three (Joanna) or even more syllables.

For example, the word "a" is a one-syllable word containing one vowel. The word "abrogate" is considered a multi-syllabic word containing three syllables "ab," "ro," and "gate."

1

Some words begin with a prefix. A prefix is a common beginning for a group of words. Some prefixes are "trans-," "non-," and "un-" Some words end in a suffix. A suffix is a common ending for a group of words. Some suffixes are "-ness," "-ing," and "-ism."

A derivative of a word is a word that is formed by changing its tense. For example, the past tense of the word "snow" is "snowed." The plural and/or possessive forms of words are also considered derivatives.

A "short form" is a quicker, easier way of writing a word. For example, the short form for "the" is the final -T. A "phrase" is a group of words that have a "short form." For example, the phrase "at the time" is written TEMT.

To write a word "phonetically" means to write a word as you hear it. For example, in the word "cat" you hear the "k" sound and would therefore write "kat."

In Realwrite, you write words phonetically; however, in some instances you also consider how a word is spelled. For example, you would write the word "hay" as "HAY" and you would write the word "hey" as "HEY."

In the accompanying lessons in this *DrillBook* you will build upon the concepts that are taught in the *LessonBook*. It is important that you learn the principles as they are presented because they will help you in your career as a realtime writer.

Beginning Exercise

☞ Place an "L" next to the word if the vowel is "long." Place an "S" next to the word if the vowel is "short." Suggested answers can be found on page 140. <u>There is no taped dictation for this drill.</u>

fan ____	ran ____	rain ____	sign ____	ten _S_	teen _L_
temp ____	boat ____	light _L_	sight _L_	pure ____	muse ____
heat ____	soap ____	drape ____	dap ____	fright ____	fit ____
site ____	sit ____	dope ____	dip ____	send ____	mend ____
store ____	bore ____	rap ____	rape ____	hit ____	owe ____
pen ____	been ____	bean ____	lit ____	stock ____	tow ____

☞ Fill in the blanks with examples of words:

✓ 5 examples of words that contain the long a:

rake _____ _____ _____ _____

✓ 5 examples of words that contain the long e:

heat _____ _____ _____ _____

✓ 5 examples of words that contain the long i:

right _____ _____ _____ _____

✓ 5 examples of words that contain the long o:

boat _____ _____ _____ _____

✓ 5 examples of words that contain the long u:

pure _____ _____ _____ _____

✓ 5 different examples of prefixes for words:

trans _____ _____ _____ _____

✓ 5 different examples of suffixes for words:

-ing _____ _____ _____ _____

✓ 5 examples of one syllable words:

stow _____ _____ _____ _____

✓ 5 examples of two syllable words:

walking _____ _____ _____ _____

✓ 5 examples of words containing three or more syllables:

abrogate _____ _____ _____ _____

due Wed. group B.

_HW._

Word Drill

In the *Realwrite LessonBook* you have been writing a series of letters or combinations of letters (for example PW-A-B). In some cases these letter combinations formed a word (for example BAEUB is the word "babe"). In this book you will expand upon this concept of writing different combinations that form words.

☞ Practice the following until you can write them without hesitation:

a AEU (1)	ad AD	bad PWAD
babe PWAEUB	beg PWEG	dad TKAD
deaf TKEF	fad TPAD	feed TPAOED
hag HAG	ah AFD	aid AEUD
bag PWAG	bed PWED	bead PWAOED
deed TKAOED	egg EG	fed TPED
gag TKPWAG	head HED	hah HAFD

(1) The article "a" is always written as a long "a"; this is to distinguish it from the prefix "a-" which will be written as a short "a."

Remember the sounding rule for long vowels. If the English word contains the sound of the vowel itself, it is long.

vowel	long vowels	short vowels
a	paid	pad
o	road	rod
i	ride	rid
e	read	red
u	crude	crud

Name and Number Drill

Names and numbers will always play an important part in your skill as court and realtime reporters. Begin now to make an effort to write all names numbers without hesitation. Mastering this aspect of your skill now will be a great help to you when you begin your career.

☞ Practice the following until you can write them without hesitation:

Abe AEUB	Ed ED	Deb TKEB	1	9

Short Form Drill

Some words are written quickly and smoothly by using a "short form" that represents the word. For example, the short form for the word "about" is the initial B (PW-). Whenever you hear the word "about," strike the initial PW-; and whenever you see the initial PW-, read the word "about."

☞ Practice the following until you can write them without hesitation:

about PW-	did TK- (-D in phrases)	of -F	he HAE (E in phrases)
be -B	if TP-	had H (-FD in phrases)	

Phrase Drill

A phrase can be considered a short form for a series of words. One phrase may take the place of two or more English words. For example, the phrase "about a" is written by the single stroke PWAEU; that is, PW- for "about" and "AEU" for "a" all combined together in one stroke.

☞ Practice the following until you can write them without hesitation:

had a HAEU (1)	if a TPAEU	did a TKAEU	about a PWAEU	
he did HAED (2)	he had HAEFD	did he TKHE (3)	had he HE (2)	if he TPE

(1) In phrases, the article "a" is always long.
(2) Use the short form HAE for "he" at beginning of a phrase (he did = HAED). Use the short form E for "he" at end of a phrase (had he = HE).
(3) The TKHE is written to avoid a conflict; practice the TKH- together and then add the E so you can write TKHE (DHE) together.

Practical Exercise

Write the sentences at least ten times for practice and then write them one more time to check over your accuracy. READ your notes carefully, circle any errors in your notes, and go back and correctly practice the words that gave you problems.

☞ Practice the following until you can write without hesitation (phases are underscored):

a bad bag (hp means home position)
a dead egg (hp)
he had a bead (hp)
if a hag had a dad (hp)
Ed had a bad egg (hp)
ah hah (hp)
be bad (hp)
he did a deed (hp)

a bad gag (hp)
about a bed (hp)
Abe had a bag of feed (hp)
be a bad hag (hp)
if Deb did beg (hp)
he had a fad about Deb (hp)
bead of feed (hp)
a babe fed (hp)

Word Drill

☞ Practice the following until you can write them without hesitation:

I AOEU (1)	bid PWEUD	badge PWAPBLG	jag SKWRAG
jig SKWREUG	hi HAOEU	big PWEUG	jab SKWRAB
jade SKWRAEUD	hide HAOEUD	guide TKPWAOEUD	die TKAOEU
back PWABG	him HEUPL	maid PHAEUD	gauge TKPWAEUPBLG
age AEUPBLG	like HRAOEUBG	me PHAE	made PHAED (2)
came KAEUPL	ache AEUBG	ill EUL	bail PWAEUL
lie HRAOEU	aim AEUPL	bake PWAEUBG	bell PWEL
bike PWAOEUBG	deck TKEBG	cab KAB	cage KAEUPBLG
lad HRAD	led HRED	deal TKAOEL	kid KEUD
lab HRAB	lag HRAG	leg HREG	ledge HREPBLG
leaf HRAOEF	ham HAPL	hem HEPL	jack SKWRABG
lead HRAOED	mad PHAD	hail HAEUL	hill HEUL
jail SKWRAEUL	jam SKWRAPL	gem SKWREPL	cake KAEUBG
kick KEUBG	kill KEUL	mill PHEUL	mile PHAOEUL

(1) The pronoun "I" is written with a long I (AOEU)
(2) In later lessons you will learn that it is necessary to distinguish between two words that sound the same but have different meanings and spellings. This is done in order to make realtime writing and instant translation (closed captioning) more accurate. You will learn the rules in later chapters.

Name and Number Drill

☞ Practice the following until you can write them without hesitation:

Lee HRAOE	Dale TKAEUL	Jill SKWREUL	Jim SKWREUPL	Meg PHEG
Kim KEUPL	Bill PWEUL	Jake SKWRAEUBG	2	8

Short Form Drill

☞ Practice the following until you can write them without hesitation:

can K (-BG)	am -PL	will HR-	come KPH-	bill PW-L	little HREUL

☞ Practice the following until you can write them without hesitation:

I can AOEUBG (1)	I did AOEUD	I had AOEUFD	I am AOEUPL	he can HAEBG
can I KEU	did I TKEU	had I HEU	will I HREU	can he KE
can a KAEU	if a TPAEU	had a HAEU	will a HRAEU	will he HRE

(1) In phrases, use the long "I" (AOEU) if the phrase begins with the pronoun "I"; if the phrase ends in the pronoun "I" use the short "I" (EU).

Write the following sentences at least ten times for practice and then write them one more time to check over your accuracy. READ your notes carefully, circle any errors in your notes, and go back and correctly practice the words that gave you problems. Write the home position STPH-FPLT (hp) after each sentence:

☞ Practice the following until you can write them without hesitation (phases are underscored).

Dale had a deck (hp)
Jim had a cake
he can bake a cake if he will
Ed made a cage

Jill did a leg kick
He can feed Meg a jam cake
I can bake a ham
can he hide

deal him a bad deck
he came back
can a lad be like me
a maid made a big bed
a cab had a big bell

Meg had a bike
a kid had jam
Kim did kick Ed
he made me mad about a bad deed

Will I feed Ed a cake
Can I make a bell
I had a headache
will he bill me

hi Lee
I came back
if he can he can
Jill made a deal about a cab
he did like me

UNIT 2
DRILL IV (Lessons 7-8)

Word Drill

☞ Practice the following until you can write them without hesitation:

and APBD (1)	man PHAPB	men PHEPB	line HRAOEUPB	no TPHOE
an APB	find TPAOEUPBD	name TPHAEUPL	end EPBD (1)	off OF
old OELD (2)	go TKPWOE	nab TPHAB	nail TPHAEUL	need TPHAOED
home HOEPL	own OEPB	nag TPHAG	neck TPHEBG	nod TPHOD
non TPHOPB	fan TPAPB	cane KAEUPB	den TKEPB	mean PHAOEPB
ban PWAPB	gain TKPWAEUPB	lane HRAEUPB	hen HEPB	bin PWEUPB
kin KEUPB	cone KOEPB	bone PWOEPB	mine PHAOEUPB	dine TKAOEUPB
gin SKWREUPB	phone TPOEPB	gone TKPWOPB	fine TPAOEUPB	her HER
pad PAD	pair PAEUR	pipe PAOEUP	pole POEL	more PHOR
pack PABG	pain PAEUPB	pill PEUL	quack KWABG	quick KWEUBG
rag RAG	rape RAEUP	roam ROEPL	map PHAP	quill KWEUL
rain RAEUPB	red RED	beer PWAOER	cape KAEUP	deep TKAOEP
rip REUP	fire TPAOEUR	keep KAOEP	here HAOER	nor TPHOR

(1) Practice of multi-consonants will come later; for now, practice the -PBD ending.
(2) Practice the -LD ending.

Name and Number Drill

☞ Practice the following until you can write them without hesitation:

Ned TPHED	Dan TKAPB	Jan SKWRAPB	Ben PWEPB
Rick REUBG	Nick TPHEUBG	Don TKOPB	Jane SKWRAEUPB
Ken KEPB	Ron ROPB	3	2
8	7	1	9

Short Form Drill

☞ Practice the following until you can write them without hesitation:

do TKAO	in TPH	even AOEFPB (1)	only OEPBL (2)	help HEP
from TPR-	after AFR-	under TKER		on O
into TPHAO	many PH-PB	could KO (-BGD)	are R (-R)	or R-R
before PW-FR	number PWER	been PW-PB		

(1) Practice writing the final -FPB together before attempting to write the word, then combine it with the long E (AOE) to write AOEFPB.
(2) Practice writing the PBL, then add the long O (OE).

Phrase Drill

☞ Practice the following until you can write them without hesitation:

could I KOEU	could he KOE	I could AOEUBGD (1)	he could HAEBGD

(1) Practice writing the -BGD together, then add the long I (AOEU).

Practical Exercise

Write the following sentences at least ten times for practice and then write them one more time to check over your accuracy. READ your notes carefully, circle any errors in your notes, and go back and correctly practice the words that gave you problems. Write the home position STPH-FPLT (hp) after each sentence:

☞ Practice the following until you can write them without hesitation (phases are underscored).

a man had a cap of big red beer (hp)
a little man did a fine job
did he rip a quill pen
I even make a quick cake
Dale and Ned are gone

I had a pill and Jan had a gin
mom and I are in need of help
Rick or Rob will go
come here and fan a fire
I go and he came

Ken could only back a deal
a map of a home will help
he did keep Ben and Meg from here
I mean I make a big cake
Deb and Don are here

dad and I are mad
if I help him will he help me
Kim or Nick had gone
come here and make a deal
I do little in jail

9

Ned could find a pack of feed
He can go under
I am on a big red cab
Abe and Jan and Ken and Jill
I need help and I need quick help

9 men or 7 men or 3 men
a kid and 4 men are gone
a dog had a bone
her phone had a bad bell
do I do a job

I can go before or after
I am red and I am on fire
I mean I am in a big red cab
Dale or Nick or Meg or Jim
a number of men are here

2 men are here and 1 kid
I nag a man on a phone
come here dog and pick a bone
I had a red cap
do I like her

Word Drill (Part I)

☞ Practice the following until you can write them without hesitation:

sack SABG	safe SAEUF	sale SAEL (1)	sat SAT
see SAOE	sad SAD	sail SAEUL (1)	same SAEUPL
save SAEUFB	seed SAOED	seat SAOET	seen SAOEPB
set SET	gas TKPWAS	face TPAEUS	seem SAOEPL
sell SEL	sin SEUPB	pass PAS	race RAEUS
lease HRAOES	peace PAES (1)	mice PHAOEUS	loss HROS
dose TKOES	piece PAOES (1)	niece TPHAOES	nice TPHAOEUS
boss PWOS	miss PHEUS	bat PWAT	hat HAT
fate TPAEUT	date TKAEUT	late HRAEUT	cat KAT
sat SAT	rate RAEUT	gate TKPWAEUT	bet PWET
get TKPWET	jet SKWRET	feet TPAOET	meet PHAOET
hit HEUT		let HRET	heat HAOET
sit SEUT	fit TPEUT	fight TPAOEUGT (2)	sight SAOEUGT
hot HOT		coat KOET	right RAOEUGT
site SAOEUT	got TKPWOT	lot HROT	quote KWOET
its EUTS	said SAEUD	not TPHOT	at AT
them THEPL	too TAO	so SOE	to TO
but PWUT	than THAPB	time TAOEUPL	put PUT

(1) Note the realtime distinctions for writing "sale" and "sail," "peace" and "piece."
(2) All words that end in "ight" are written with the AOEUGT at the ending.

Number Drill

Write the number using the number bar and the appropriate letter key. Hit the crack between the home position key and the number bar quickly and cleanly.

☞ Practice the following until you can write them without hesitation:

4	3	2	8	6	7
1	9	1	8	7	2
3	7	6	1	4	9

Short Form Drill (Part I)

☞ Practice the following until you can write them without hesitation:

is S- (-S in phrases)	also HR-S	that THA	this THEU	there THR-
not TPHOT (-PB)	first TPEURT	some SPH-	the -T	it T-
they THE	their THEUR	take TAE		

Phrase Drill (Part I)

☞ Practice the following until you can write them without hesitation:

is it ST-	is that STHA	is there STHR-	is the S-T	is this STHEU
is not S-PB	some of SPH-F	some are SPH-R	that the THAT	it is T-S
about the PW-T	if the TP-T	can the K-T	did the TK-T	of the -FT
will the HR-T	on the OT	in the TPH-T	into the TPHAOT	from the TPR-T
are the R-T	that are THAR	they are THER	there are THR-R	cannot K-PB
there is THR-S	will not HR-PBT			

Practical Exercise (Part I)

Write the following sentences at least ten times for practice and then write them one more time to check your accuracy. READ your notes carefully, circle any errors in your notes, and go back and practice the words that gave you problems. Write the home position STPH-FPLT (hp) after each sentence:

☞ Practice the following until you can write them without hesitation (phases are underscored).

is it safe to be in a car
is the fight at the same time
can the man at the site see the cat
a jet will pass the car in the race
I got a lot of mice at the sale

is it hot at the race or not
many feet make quick time
they are gone and not at home
he hit him in the face at the fight
Ron will sail off into the night

can the boss sell the hat to the man
the niece ate a piece of hot pie
there are more than that
Meg cannot and Dale cannot
the heat is hot so take the coat off

it is so so be it
if the bat is right hit it
some are and some are not
I can and Don can but Ben cannot
I am the first to take the seat

I got gas for the jet but it is gone
if there is no quote then there is not
save some seed for the sale
lease a seat for the date
their feet will not race

Is there a quote to quote or not
a cat put the bat in the hat
a sin is a sin and that is sad
it is late and there is no time
their cat ate the mice

12

I too am about to go to meet Ned

I also am about to go to meet Jan

<u>this is</u> a quote <u>about the</u> fate of a hat

<u>will the</u> loss be too little or too big

a sack of feed is safe from the rain

<u>it is</u> their first time <u>in a</u> car

a nice man said not to put it there

sit or set or sat but take a seat

<u>is that the</u> man to meet or not

<u>did the</u> lease make peace

meet me so <u>I can</u> see the nice niece

<u>it is</u> not time so I <u>cannot</u> go there

Word Drill (Part II)

☞ Practice the following until you can write them without hesitation:

dud TKUD	tug TUG	luck HRUBG	pull PUL
fun TPUPB	dude TKAOUD	mug PHUG	full TPUL
gum TKPWUPL	gun TKPWUPB	bus PWUS	nut TPHUT
van SRAPB	vet SRET	vote SROET	but PWUT
tube TAOUB	vine SRAOEUPB	vice SRAOEUS	vain SRAEUPB
save SAEUFB	waive WAEUFB	give TKPWEUFB	live HREUFB
dive TKAOEUFB	pave PAEUFB	wave WAEFB	five TPAOEUFB
live HRAOEUFB	love HROFB	dove TKOFB	wade WAEUD
war WAR	ware WAER	well WEL	dove TKOFB
wage WAEUPBLG	wake WAEUBG	wear WAEUR	wet WET
week WAOEBG	wig WEUG	wide WAOEUD	wire WAOEUR
jaw SKWRAFRP	weed WAOED	win WEUPB	wine WAOEUPB
woke WOEBG	law HRAFRP	saw SAFRP	few TPEFRP
view SREFRP	low HROEFRP	sow SOEFRP	dew TKEFRP
sew SEFRP	bow PWOEFRP	mow PHOEFRP	tow TOEFRP
how HOFRP	pow POFRP	now TPHOFRP	wow WOFRP
up UP	us US	we WE	who WHO
new TPHEFRP	went WEPBT	while WHAOEUL	does TKUZ

Short Form Drill (Part II)

☞ Practice the following until you can write them without hesitation:

have SR (-FB)	with W-	were WR-	when WH-	where WHR-
was WA	which WHEU	would WO	what WHA	very SRE-
between TWAOEPB	write WREU	will HR (-FRP)		

13

Phrase Drill (Part II)

☞ Practice the following until you can write them without hesitation:

we are WER	we did WAED (1)	we had WEFD	we can WEBG
we have WEFB	have you SRAU	have I SREU	I have AOEUFB
with you WAU	which is WHEUS	were you WRAU	was he WAE
was the WAT	I will AOEUFRP	they will THEFRP	he will HAEFRP
what is WHAS	when is WH-S	which is WHEUS	when are WH-R
where are WHR-R	where the WHR-T	do you TKOU (2)	did you TKAU (2)
if you TPAU (2)	will you HRAU (2)		

(1) The short form WAED is used for "we did" to avoid a conflict with "wed" (WED).
(2) All phrases that end in the word "you" are written with the AU except do you TKOU.

Practical Exercise (Part II)

Write the following sentences at least ten times for practice and then write them one more time to check your accuracy. READ your notes carefully, circle any errors in your notes, and go back and practice the words that gave you problems. Write the home position STPH-FPLT (hp) after each sentence:

☞ Practice the following until you can write them without hesitation (listen for the phrases).

he was a dude while he was here
we are to view the vote
where do you mow
I saw five live men
there was a fight between us

he will pick a nut off the vine
have you a piece of gum
Joe saw the man tow the car
Was it Jim or her who hit him
I now pave a road with tar

while here see the van
where is it
a van is not a bus but a bus is a van
the tube was full of gum
the law is up

they will save the dove from harm
were we here or were we there
give me a full mug of beer
I am very sick this week

now he is a dud
I dive into the mud
how do you mow
a dove went into the wire
I will sow a row of vine

I love to pick a weed from the vine
I live with my dog and cat
Who went in while I was here
we cannot sow the seed here
he will pave the road with rock

what is it a car or a van or a bus
a wet weed is what I saw when I dove
I dive while he dove
he did well
but I can do what I want to do

a pow wow is not a war
wear a wet wig and we will waive
a new law will give me luck
we are us and they are us but I am me

14

UNIT 3
DRILL VI (Lessons 11-12)

Word Drill

☞ Practice the following until you can write them without hesitation:

exam SKPAPL	except SKPEPT (1)	excess SKPES	extra STRA (1)
x-ray SKPRAFPL	expect SKPEBGT	exit SKPEUT	exact SKPABGT
tax TAFRPB	wax WAFRPB	lax HRAFRPB	sex SEFRPB
ox OFRPB	fox TPOFRPB	you KWROU	year KWRAOER
your KWROUR	yet KWRET	yup KWRUP	bay PWAFPL (2)
say SAFPL	may PHAFPL	pay PAFPL	way WAFPL
boy PWOFPL	toy TOFPL	guy TKPWUFPL	buy PWUFPL
why WH-FPL	yes KWRES	as AZ	his HEUZ
has HAZ (3)	use AOUZ	phase TPAEUZ	rose ROEZ
rise RAOEUZ	tease TAOEZ	zip SKPWEUP	zap SKPWAP
zig SKPWEUG	zag SKPWAG	zone SKPWOEPB	zoo SKPWAO

(1) The SKP is used for the "ex," "exp," "exc," and "exh," prefixes; "ext" prefixes begin with ST.
(2) Words that are spelled with a vowel before the "y" are written as they appear in English as in say (SAFPL), key (KEFPL), and guy (TKPWUFPL)
(3) "Has" can be written in phrases by using the initial Z- (SKPW-) or final -Z (-Z).

Name and Number Drill

☞ Practice the following until you can write them without hesitation:

Kay KAFPL	Ray RAFPL	Fay TPAFPL	Roy ROFPL
Rex REFRPB	Max PHAFRPB	Zeb SKPWEB	Rose ROEZ
5	0	19	29
37	46	48	50

Short Form Drill

☞ Practice the following until you can write them without hesitation:

any TPHEU	eye EFPL	because PWAUZ	done TKOEPB	business PWEUZ

15

☞ Practice the following until you can write them without hesitation:

you KWROU (1)	if you TPAU	could you KAOU	did you TKAU
had you HAU	have you SRAU	can you KAU	when you WHU
from you TPRAU	will you HRAU	were you WRAU	that you THAU
with you WAU	would you WAOU	about you PWAU	are you RAU
you are UR	you could UBGD	you did UD	you had UFD
you have UFB	you can UBG	you will UFRP	
yes, sir KWREUR	no, sir TPHEUR	yes, ma'am KWREPL	no, ma'am TPHOEPL

(1) "You" is written KWROU. If a phrase begins with "you," use U; if it ends in "you," use AU.

☞ Practice the following until you can write them without hesitation (phrases are underscored):

he will take an exam
will you pay the extra tax
with your excess you can buy a toy
did you say yes sir or no sir
what sex is the new born babe

he said yes ma'am then he said no
he said no ma'am then he said yes
did you see an ox or a fox or a cow
would you phase out the tax
where will you exit

you could go to a new zone
I went zip zap on my way home
you are able to pay all except 5
did you say the play was about a boy
I will buy you a new toy if you go

what year is this any way
he will tease his boss
my eye is sore because I cry
you can see if you see
yes or no what do you say

are you to rise
do not be lax on your tax
pay a fee if you buy a toy

you will expect to see him
were you to pay the boy
did he say yes or yup
use the wax on the floor
would you zap an egg for me

if you could see him now
why are you at the zoo
a guy said it was a dog
I had an x-ray done on my head
where could you go

he went zig zag in the road
you did what
had you done any business with him
may I see your eye
the rose was red because it was red

you are here yet you are not
will you use your pay
I cry because my eye is sore
you can see if you see
you have to rise and shine

he has yet to say the word bay
I will say the word bay now
do not pay a tax

Word Drill

☞ Review the following until you can write them without hesitation:

stick STEUBG	stuck STUBG	stop STOP	stay STAFPL
stain STAEUPB	able AEUBL	table TAEUBL	double TKOUBL
state STAEUT	stable STAEUBL	part PART	warm WARPL
mobile PHOEBL	rubble RUBL	art ART	start START
fort TPORT	wart WART	dart TKART	arm ARPL
harm HARPL	storm STORPL	worm WORPL	germ SKPWERPL
outcome OUT/KPH-	doctor TKOBG/TOR	carpet KAR/PET (1)	window WEUPB/TKOEFRP
too TAO	spare SPAEUR	spot SPOT	speak SPAOEBG
spend SPEPBD	spud SPUD	spoke SPOEBG	raffle RAFL
waffle WAFL	baffle PWAFL	duffel TKUFL	muffle PHUFL
ruffle RUFL	curl KURL	pearl PERL	girl TKPWEURL
whirl WHEURL	viral SRAOEURL	barrel PWAEURL	
mountain PHOUPB/TAEUPB	highway HAOEUFD/WAEFPL	airplane AEUR/PHRAEPB	driveway TKRAOEUFB/WAEFPL
pool PAOL	door TKAOR	all AUL	tall TAUL
law HRAFRP	saw SAFRP	awe AFRP	

(1) In later lessons you will learn an important realtime principal that deals with making a distinction between words that are considered one word (carpet) as opposed to words that are considered two words (car and pet). For now, learn the phonetics and you will learn the principal later.

Name and Number Drill

☞ Review the following until you can write them without hesitation:

Denver TKEPB/SRER		Johnson SKWROPB/SOEPB		Newport TPHEFRP/POERT		Cadillac KAD/HRABG		Paul PAUL	
99	EU9	74	4EU7	42	2EU4	33	3EU	36	36
71	1EU7	82	2EU8	14	14	74	4EU7	11	1EU
55	5EU	50	50	13	13	64	4EU6	49	49
77	EU7	10	10	90	0EU9	70	0EU7	45	45

17

Short Form Drill

☞ Review the following until you can write them without hesitation:

ago AOG	evidence EFD	identify AOEUF	half HAF	apply PHREU
behalf PWAF	figure TP-G	passenger PAEPBG	behind PWEFD	gentleman SKWRA
gentlemen SKWRE	being PWAOEG	gym TKPWEUPL	damage TKAPBLG	almost HR-PL
actual TAOUL	aloud HR-D	along HR-G	Mr. PHR-	after AFR
already HR-RD	also HR-S	among PHOPBG	basic PWEUBG	become PW-BG
remain R-PL				
acknowledge ABG/TPHOPBLG	applicable PHREUBG	emergency PH-PBLG	detail TKAEL	enclose KHR-

Punctuation Drill

☞ Review the following until you can write them without hesitation:

the period (.)	-FPLT	the comma (,)	-RBGS

Practical Exercise

Beginning in this Drill, all Practical Exercises are counted in group of 20 words per slash (/). Use the chart found in the *Instructor's Manual* for dictation purposes.

☞ Practice the following until you can write them without hesitation (all phases are underscored):

1. Paul got sick from a worm that he ate.
2. I won a barrel at the raffle in Newport.
3. A girl with / a curl got sick.
4. He had a viral germ, but it is almost gone.
5. He will enclose a note in the bag. /

6. The duffel bag could not fit all of it.
7. A leaf fell in the highway.
8. An airplane almost / ran into the cab.
9. I spoke to the tall girl.
10. A ruffle is not a muffle.

11. I was in awe / because of the emergency.
12. I cannot tell you what I saw.
13. The law is the law.
14. I saw a Cadillac / on the highway.
15. You go into the pool.

16. The door is stuck.
17. I had to spend time at home with / Kim.
18. I became mad when Paul ate my pie.
19. We will go to the mountain to see.
20. I saw a / spot in the road.

21. The spare tire will not fit.
22. It was warm after the storm.
23. Half of the gentlemen / had a germ.
24. I was able to see the outcome of the race.
25. My part was to start the race. /

26. The rain will acknowledge the storm.
27. 30 is the figure.
28. The figure is not 50, but 20.
29. Jim had no / evidence.
30. The stain on the carpet would not come out.

31. The wax was hard.
32. Is there a car in the driveway. /
33. The doctor cut off the wart on the arm.
34. He sat in the gym.
35. He broke his arm.

36. The damage / to the car was bad.
37. He had to fix it because he had to go to work.
38. The passenger in the / car got stuck in the window.
39. I am in a play about a man who ate a pie.
40. I hurt / my head on a table.

UNIT 4
DRILL VIII (Lessons 15-16)

Word Drill

☞ Review the following until you can write them without hesitation:

ship SHEUP	shore SHOR (1)	sure SHAOUR	show SHOEFRP
shut SHUT	shy SH-FPL	apt APT	opt OPT
kept KEPT	dark TKARBG	spark SPARBG	work WORBG
cork KORBG	jerk SKWRERBG	mark PHARBG	hardware HARD/WAER
carport KAR/POERT	pencil PEPB/SEUL	airport AEUR/POERT	fork TPORBG
how HOFRP	now TPHOFRP	cow KOFRP	town TOUPB
clown KHROUPB	oil OEUL	soil SOEUL	royal ROEUL
toy TOFPL	soy SOFPL	joy SKWROFPL	small SPHAUL
smart SPHART	smoke SPHOEBG	smack SPHABG	smut SPHUT
aft AFT	craft KRAFT	draft TKRAFT	raft RAFT
rift REUFT	soft SOFT	software SOFT/WAER	compute KOPL/PAOUT
message PHES/KWRAPBLG	briefcase BRAOEF/KAES		

(1) As a general rule, use the short "o" before the consonant "r," unless a conflict occurs with another word.

Name and Number Drill

☞ Review the following until you can write them without hesitation:

Filmore TPEUL/PHOER	Newark TPHEFRP/KWRARBG	Robert ROB/KWRERT	Wilson WEUL/SOEPB
42 2EU4	26 26	97 7EU9	50 50
182 1/H-PBD/2EU8	239 2/H-PBD/39	702 7/H-PBD/9 2	12 12
505 5/H-PBD/5	999 9/H-PBD/EU9	85 5EU8	444 4/H-PBD/4EU
732 7/H-PBD/2EU	821 8/H-PBD/12EU	361 3/H-PBD/1EU6	87 7EU8
525 5/H-PBD/25	691 6/H-PBD/1EU9	250 2/H-PBD/50	431 4/H-PBD/13EU

Short Form and Phrase Drill

☞ Review the following until you can write them without hesitation:

envelope TPHEFL	family TPAPL	gallon TKPW-L	follow TPOL
identify AOEUF	immediate PHAOED	important PORPBT	item T-PL
labor HRAEUB	legal HRAOEL	major PHAEUPBLG	done TKOEPB
manage PH-G	mechanic PH-BG	memo PHEPL	manufacture PH-F
maybe PHAEUB	member PHEB	do you TKOU	how many HOUPL

Punctuation Drill

☞ Review the following until you can write them without hesitation:

the question mark (?)	STPH-	new paragraph	PA-RBGS

Practical Exercise

☞ Practice the following until you can write them without hesitation:

Robert Wilson will manage a shop that will deal in the manufacture of hardware and software. He will be / able to compute any figure that you give to him. If you would like to compute, send them a memo. / If you need a pen or pencil to write the memo, let me get it for you. Do you need / help?

The new shop will also tell you if there is soil in your oil. This may seem odd, but it / is so. Do you have a briefcase you can put all of this in? If you do, make / sure that you give it to Robert. He will show you what to do.

Do you like to do art / or craft? I like craft. We did not have class because of the smoke. I am smart in art class, / but I like craft class first. It is a joy to go to class.

Do you like to sail on / a ship, or do you like to sit on a shore? My wife and I like to sit on shore. / It is important to me to labor and to work hard at what I do. My family and I all / like to work hard.

My hardware and software are not able to compute. I had to take them to the / shop to fix them. When I got to the shop, the man told me that I had to take them to Newark. / I did not want to drive because I only had 1 gallon of gas.

Do you want me to get / my hardware and software to Newark? It will not fit into an envelope. I will follow what you say, but / it is important for me to get this done before noon.

How many men will it take to lift up / the hardware? I will see if you and your family can help. What time will you be here?

I have / to go to the airport at 7. Will you meet me at the airport? I hope to be / able to pick up my hardware and software on the plane. If I cannot, will you pick it up for / me? I cannot drive my car in the dark.

Word Drill

☞ Review the following until you can write them without hesitation:

chart KHART	chat KHAT	chief KHAOEF	cheat KHAOET
chime KHAOEUPL	cheer KHAOER	chip KHEUP	chain KHAEUPB
chair KHAEUR	chalk KHAUBG	charm KHARPL	chase KHAEUS
chew KHEFRP	chow KHOFRP	sheet SHAOET	shirt SHEURT
shine SHAOEUPB	shag SHAG	shin SHEUPB	shoe SHAOU
shade SHAEUD	shake SHAEUBG	shall SHAL	shame SHAEUPL
timed TAOEUPLD	lived HREUFB/AED	mixed PHEUFRPBD	ruled RAOULD
opted OPT/AED	raided RAEUD/AED	zapped SKPWAPD	voted SROET/AED
jailed SKWRAEULD	tried TRAOEUD	vowed SROFRPD	seated SAOET/AED
razzed RAZ/AED	stayed STAFPLD	why WH-FPL	raced RAEUS/AED
dared TKAEURD	dated TKAEUT/AED	dazed TKAEUZ/AED	dined TKAOEUPB/AED
faced TPAEUS/AED	faded TPAEUD/AED	never TPHEFR	over OEFR
those THOEZ	hour HOUR	should SHOULD	wear WAEUR
caused KAUZ/AED	spell SPEL	fizzes TPEUZ/AEZ	fear TPAOER
bars PWARZ	seats SAOETS	girls TKPWEURLZ	cars KARZ
passes PAS/AEZ	doors TKAORZ	houses HOUS/AEZ	boys PWOFPLZ
cans KAPBZ	kisses KEUS/AEZ	coats KOETS	roses ROEZ/AEZ
tabs TABZ	pads PADZ	scare SKAEUR	arms ARPLZ
tables TAEUBLZ	arts ARTS	sky SK-FPL	farms TPARPLZ
bubbles PWUBLZ	parts PARTS	skip SKEUP	storms STORPLZ
stables STAEUBLZ	darts TKARTS	one WUPB (1)	looked HRAOBGD
near TPHAOER	rock ROBG	star STAR	stage STAEUPBLG
name TPHAEUPL	band PWAPBD	hear HAER	own OEPB
horses HORS/AEZ	ice AOEUSZ	cows KOWZ	spilled SPEULD
bag PWAG	fell TPEL	move PHOFB	months PHOPBZ (2)
enjoyed EPB/SKWROFPLD	headache HED/KWRAEUBG	moonshine PHAOPB/AE/SHAOEUPB (3)	

(1) The word "won" is written WOPB; "one" is written WUPB.
(2) The short form for "month" is PHOPB; the plural "months" is written PHOPBZ
(3) The AE between PHAOPB and SHAOEUPB is necessary to connect the two words to form one word.

Number Drill

☞ Practice the following until you can write them without hesitation:

34,556	34/THZ/5/HPBD/56	72,436	2EU7/THZ/4/HPBD/36
50,471	50/THZ/4/HPBD/1EU7	12,912	12/THZ/9/HPBD/12
31,070	13EU/THZ/70	5,418	5/THZ/4/HPBD/18

Short Form and Phrase Drill

☞ Review the following until you can write them without hesitation:

minimum PHEUPL	month PHOPB	must PHU	most PHO
possible POB	alone HR-PB	used AOUDZ	monthly PHOL
public PUBL	perform PEFRPL	sister STER	again TKPWEPB
bill PW-L	automobile AOBL	bottom PW-PL	did not TK-PBT
bills PW-LZ	do not TKAOPB	does not TKUPBT	could not KOPBT
billed PW-LD	began TKPWAPB	begun TKPW-PB	begin TKPWEUPB

Practical Exercise

☞ Practice the following until you can write them without hesitation:

Why did they put him in jail when he did not pay his bills? The 3 gentlemen in the store / told him he did not have to pay. He was sure he could pay them monthly, but he could not. / By the time he got the bills paid, he was broke. The man told him to work for 1 month / to try to pay it all off, but he got sick and got a germ. He is now at home / in bed for 6 months; he cannot work at all.

Will you pay the bills for him? Ken said he / would help. He tried to use his spare figures, but it would not work. He went to the mountain to / see if he could get more, but he could not. It was a real emergency; he did not want to / stay on the mountain because it got dark and it looked like a storm in the sky.

One way that / he could earn some is to sell his 2 farms and 6 stables. They have over 500 cows and about / 16,400 horses. If they sold the farm, they could pay the bills. One more way to pay the bills / would be to hire a rock star to come on stage at their barn. They could hire Kisses and Roses. / If they did, all of the seats would be sold out.

They could sell over 15,000 seats and make / a lot. They could also have a race to see who would be first. If they had a race, I / would not be able to begin because I broke my arm and my leg when I fell off a horse. / I began to cry, but I did not because it did not hurt that bad. I did cry for help. /

A gentleman from Denver by the name of Rick Johnson came to help me. The public said he was a / good help. Mr. Johnson vowed to help me all he could. My sister and I went to the doctor to / see what the damage was; it was quite bad. I broke my arm, my leg, and my head.

I hear / chimes in my head all day. I also hear a cheer, but that is my sister. She says I should / chat more. I tried, but I did not like to chat.

The chief doctor told me to stay near him. / Most of the time I can, but I must do more. The doctor lived near a shop that sold / zig zag bars. I had 22 zig zag bars in 1 day. Now, I am sick and tired of zig / zag bars.

It is important to do my work again and again. Most of the work I do I put / on a chart, but some of it I do not. I write nice; I shine; I perform well. My monthly / goal is to go 200, but I will vow to do 100. I must do all that is / possible to be sure I can write nice. I must do the minimum.

UNIT 5
DRILL X (Lessons 19-20)

Word Drill

☞ Review the following until you can write them without hesitation:

happy HAP/AEFPL	honey HOPB/AEFPL	Bobbie PWOB/KWRAOE	marry PHAEUR/AEFPL
sunny SUPB/AEFPL	baby PWAEUB/AEFPL	soapy SOEP/AEFPL	scary SKAEUR/AEFPL
committee KPHEUT/KWRAOE	jiffy SKWREUF/AEFPL	movie PHOFB/KWRAOE	spicy SPAOEUS/AEFPL
crying KR-FPL/AEG	caring KAEURG	boating PWOET/AEG	digging TKEUG/AEG
walking WAUBG/AEG	talking TAUBG/AEG	dancing TKAPBS/AEG	running RUPB/AEG
jogging SKWROG/AEG	loving HROFBG	trying TR-FPL/AEG	school SKAOL
tub TUB	dried TKRAOEUD	named TPHAEUPLD	great TKPWRAEUT
wants WAPBTS	wanted WAPBT/AED	morning PHORPB/AEG	chose KHOEZ
because PWAUZ	stopped STOPD	noon TPHAOPB	people PAOEPL
cried KRAOEUD	grows TKPWROEFRPZ	choose KHAOZ	who WHO
doll TKOL	story STOR/AEFPL	bunny PWUPB/AEFPL	Luke HRAOUBG
loves HROFBZ	told TOELD	group TKPWROUP	friend TPFREPBD
arguing ARG/AEG (1)	argued ARGD (1)	waitress WAEUT/RES	spilled SPEULD
paid PAEUD	floor TPHRAOR	close KHROES	notified TPH-FD (1)
paying PAFPLG	debt TKET	trouble TROUBL	arranged ARPBGD
appeared A/PAOERD	realize RAOEL/KWRAOEUZ	worries WOR/KWRAOEZ	forgot TPOER/TKPWOT
coffee KOF/KWRAOE	books PWAOBGZ	bills PW-LZ (1)	high HAOEUFD

(1) These words are derivatives of the short form.

Short Form and Phrase Drill

☞ Review the following until you can write them without hesitation:

engine TPH-G	engineer TPH-PBLG	enough TPHUF	examine SKP-PB
example SKP-PL	finance TP-PBS	financial TP-PBL	general SKWR-PB
gentle SKWREPBL	had not H-PBT	handle HAPBL	income TPH-BG
minute PHEUPB	money PHE	necessary TPHE	neglect TPHEG
neighbor TPHAEUB	notify TPH-F	object OB	personal PERPBL
until TPH-L	afternoon TPAOPB	accompany A/K-P	argue ARG
around ARPBD	arrange ARPBG	carry K-R	carrying K-RG
following TPOLG	notified TPH-FD		

☞ Review the following until you can write them without hesitation:

the apostrophe (')	A-RBGS	singular possessive ('s)	/AOS

Practical Exercise

☞ Practice the following until you can write them without hesitation:

The figures that you gave me will not compute. Do you have any that will? The numbers that you gave / me will compute. Do you have more numbers? My figures never seem to work out; but yours do. It makes / me happy when my figures all come out right. Do your figures work?

He will show you what to put / into your briefcase when you go on the trip. He will tell you what to do. He said to put / about 2300 pads in your case, but do not forget to take a pencil or a pen. You will / need to write a great deal.

Do you need any help in packing your briefcase? I will see if Robert / Wilson can help you. He is a man who can help you. He once took the oil out of soil / and made a lot of money. Now he is broke; but he likes to help people.

The object of the / story is: never spend a lot of money trying to get oil from soil, because if you do, you may / become broke. They did not realize what it was until they got real close. It appeared to be a real / hard job.

The waitress had a personal note from Robert saying that he could show her how to get oil from soil. / She paid him over 98,000; he never showed her. He is a cheat, and he should be put / in jail. I tried to argue; but it did not do any good. It is no use arguing with him. He appeared / to be in trouble, but he would not notify her until late afternoon. He did accompany her to the land, / but there was no oil to be found.

Now that all of the oil is gone from the soil; there / is very little to do. You could neglect to pay your bills; but if you do, the price will be / high. Who will pay your bills if you do not? I cannot; he cannot. You could sell books on how / to make coffee, but that would not get you any money. If you spilled the coffee, you could arrange to clean / it up. How are you ever going to pay your debt? Who will pay it for you? I will / not.

It was dark by the time I got home. I am sure that my wife will not chase you from / here. She loves people. It is important for her to do good work in her major, but it is / hard.

I gave a message to Joe to pick up his airplane at the airport. He got an envelope saying / to pick up his car; not his airplane. He had to talk to a lawyer to take the case to / court. There was a great deal of legal work to do.

I will see you and your family in / court. What time did you say you will be there? Some man said that court started at 12, but Joe / said 11.

Luke said he wants to be an engineer on an engine, but he will not try hard. Luke / is moving in a month. He will move to Denver to see if he can study to be an engineer. / He will have a good income, and his finances will be good.

The soapy baby stopped crying after I told / her a story about a honey bee. The bee went to school to see the boys and girls. The bee / began to fly, but I did not see it.

I began running, jogging, walking, dancing, and digging to keep fit. / The doctor will examine me and see if I am fit to go to the moon. I will go / to the moon after the doctor says I am fit.

Word Drill

☞ Review the following until you can write them without hesitation:

whale WHAEUL	whim WHEUPL	white WHAOEUT	wrap WRAP
wrong WROPBG	wheel WHAOEL	whine WHAOEUPB	whole WHOEL
wreck WREBG	while WHAOEUL	whose WHOES	wheels WHAOELZ
writ WREUT	whales WHAEULZ	wrapping WRAPG	wrapped WRAPD
amazing A/PHAEUZ/AEG	amuse A/PHAOUZ	amass A/PHAS	aloud A/HROUD
abet A/PWET	affix A/TPEUFRPB	ajar A/SKWRAR	arise A/RAOEUZ
astray A/STRAFPL	abut A/PWUT	afraid A/TPRAEUD	afar A/TPAR
alive A/HRAOEUFB	allot A/HROT	appraise A/PRAEUZ	avert A/SRERT
attack A/TABG	avow A/SROFRP	heard HAERD	fear TPAOER
rabbit RAB/KWREUT	front TPROPBT	loose HRAOS	aside A/SAOEUD
steering STAOERG	away A/WAFPL	sea SAE	Joan SKWROEPB
Jones SKWROEPBZ	scare SKAEUR	skit SKEUT	scar SKAR
thaw THAFRP	these THAOEZ	thick THEUBG	score SKOR
scale SKAEUL	scram SKRAPL	theft THEFT	those THOEZ
thin THEUPB	scream SKRAOEPL	scan SKAPB	screw SKREFRP
theme THAOEPL	them THEPL	then THEPB	letting HRET/AEG
mind PHAOEUPBD	driver TKRAOEUFR	work WORBG	tried TRAOEUD
Jennifer SKWREPB/TPER	stayed STAFPLD	locked HROBGD	cement SEPLT
harassment HA/RAS/PHAEPBT	basement PWAEUS/PHAEPBT	whinny WHAOEUPB/AEFPL	excitement SKPAOEUT/PHAEPBT
confinement KOPB/TPAOEUPB/PHAEPBT	enjoyment EPB/SKWROFPL/PHAEPBT	amazement A/PHAEUZ/PHAEPBT	fulfillment TPUL/TPEUL/PHAEPBT

Short Form and Phrase Drill

☞ Review the following until you can write them without hesitation:

better TER	company K-P	describe TKRAOEUB	employ PHROEU
writes WREUZ	carry K-R	concern KERPB	determine TKERPL
employee PHROE	writing WREUG	circumstance SEURBG	degree TKRAOE
Dr. TKR-	employer PHROEUR	written WREUPB	copy KP-FPL
payment PAEUPLT	appointment POEUPLT	estimate STEUPLT	judgment SKWRUPLT
document TKOUPLT	apartment PARPLT	equipment KW-PLT	investment SREPLT
shipment SHEUPLT	involvement SROFPLT	right RAOEUGT	brought PWROUGT
sight SAOEUGT	thought THOUGT	bought PWOUGT	tight TAOEUGT
taught TAUGT	caught KAUGT	fight TPAOEUGT	fought TPOUGT
acknowledgment ABG/TPHOPBLG/ PHAEPBT	arrangement ARPBG/PHAEPBT	requirement RAOEURPLT	employment PHROEUPLT

Contraction Drill

☞ Review the following until you can write them without hesitation:

aren't R-PBZ	can't K-PBZ	couldn't KOPBZ	didn't TK-PBZ
doesn't TKUPBZ	don't TKAOPBZ	hadn't H-PBZ	hasn't SKPW-PBZ
haven't SR-PBZ	isn't S-PBZ	shouldn't SHOUPBZ	wasn't WAEPBZ
won't WOEPBZ	wouldn't WOUPBZ	ain't AEUPBZ	

Number Drill

☞ Practice the following large numbers:

millions	billions	trillions
1,245,657	2,389,893,991	234,231,992,991,891
45,923,234	89,990,560,921	9,821,891,882,891
77,921,990	3,821,991,811	92,855,308,821,443
2,345,891	43,567,392,156	1,345,987,345,951

Practical Exercise

☞ Practice the following until you can write them without hesitation:

Kate and Ben didn't see the rock star on stage. They were unable to get near the stage because there / were 45 billion people there. It was an amazing sight to see, but the band played lousy. All of the boys and / girls screamed loud. They wanted them to get off the stage.

Didn't you say that Jerry and Jenny had pigs / and ducks, cows and horses, on their farm? I thought they grew corn and wheat. Now, I learn that they / have a stable and a barn. Do they get any enjoyment out of farming? Do they grow their own / food?

What is your estimate? What is your judgment? Do you get fulfillment or enjoyment out of going to school all / day long? Didn't you say that there were over 45 billion words to learn to write? Now that you can / write some words, don't you feel better?

Did Jan file the document? Did she use the equipment? Did she pay / the rent? Did she fix the door? Did she use a screwdriver or a hammer to fix it?

I sat in / awe and amazement at the baseball game. The score was 22 to 0 in the top of the inning. By / the end of the inning, the score was all tied up. I had to leave, so I can't say who / won. Can you tell me who won the game?

Did she cheat on the paper she wrote? If she did, / she should be sent to the chief chef. The chief chef will make her write a paper that tells about / how wrong it is to cheat. Shouldn't we cheer for her?

I am looking for a shop that sells used / parts. Can you tell me where I can find one? I need a lot of parts. Most parts can't be / found, but Jill said she can help me find mixed parts. If you buy mixed parts, you can't go / wrong.

Isn't it important to do your work? Again, I say, isn't it important to do your work? Can't you / begin to tell me? Aren't you sure? Can't you tell me? Didn't you have any clue? Shouldn't you / try to tell me? Wouldn't you like to try to tell me? Haven't you begun your work yet? Why not? Please / tell me, now.

A man in a car had a wreck with a girl in an automobile on the highway. / She turned her steering wheel one way while he turned his the same way. They collided. They are lucky they / are alive.

Whose car was it? I haven't seen them since the wreck. Are they walking and talking? What did / the crowd of people say about the wreck? Did you see the wreck?

I can't appraise it, because I didn't / see it. If I had seen it, I could tell you better what I saw, but I didn't see it. Zeb / saw the wreck, but he won't talk. He says that if he began talking, he would have to tell a lie / because he is in fear of the man. The man said that if he tells what he saw, he will stop / him. Now, Zeb is afraid. What would you do?

Word Drill

☞ Review the following until you can write them without hesitation:

collect KHREBGT	command KPHAPBD	collide KHRAOEUD	commit KPHEUT
combine KPWAOEUPB	combat KPWAT	column KHRUPL	commence KPHEPBS
comment KPHEPBT	commerce KPHERS	compete KPAOET	compress KPRES
complete KPHRAOET	complex KPHREFRPB	compose KPOEZ	suit SAOUT
drapes TKRAEUPZ	colored KHRORD	crowd KROFRPD	truck TRUBG
lawyer HROEUR	court KOURT	tickets TEUBGTS	meal PHAOEL
subtraction SUB/TRABGS	conviction KOPB/SREUBGS	audition AUD/KWREUGS	attention A/TEPBGS
admission AD/PHEUGS	compulsion KPULGS	mission PHEUGS	remission RE/PHEUGS
sensation SEPB/SAEUGS	transmission TRAPBS/PHEUGS	transaction TRAPBS/KWRABGS	invention EUPB/SREPBGS
vision SREUGS	fusion TPAOUGS	tension TEPBGS	faction TPABGS
traction TRABGS	action ABGS	diction TKEUBGS	fiction TPEUBGS
faction TPABGS	fraction TPRABGS	slow SHROEFRP	slum SHRUPL
sleep SHRAOEP	sled SHRED	slug SHRUG	shred SKHRED
shriek SKHRAOEBG	shrug SKHRUG	shrine SKHRAOEUPB	shroud SKHROUD
shrew SKHREFRP	please PHRAOES	pleas PHRAOEZ	plight PLAOEUGT
plan PHRAPB	plain PHRAEUPB	plane PHRAEPB	course KOURS
Johnny SKWROPB/AEFPL	Jackie SKWRABG/KWRAOE	audition AUD/KWREUGS	proud PROUD

Short Form Drill

☞ Review the following until you can write them without hesitation:

self SEFL	selves SEFLZ	junior SKWR-R	juror SKWROR
jury SKWRUR	injury SKWR-FPL	instruct STRUBGT	letter HRER
manager PH-R	material TAOERL	motor PHOER	manufacture PH-F
natural TPHARL	open OEP	openly OEPL	opinion P-PB
order ORD	organize ORG	police PHREUS	policeman PHRAPL
policemen PHREPL	reply PHRAOEU	apply PHREU	application PHREUBGS
condition K-PBGS	document TKOUPLT	next TPH-FRPB	second SEBGD
down TKOUFRP	ever EFR	every EFB	comfort K-FRT
documentation TKOUPLGS			

☞ Review the following until you can write them without hesitation:

itself T-/SAEFL	herself HER/SAEFL	himself HEUPL/SAEFL	myself PH-FPL/SAEFL
ourselves OUR/SAEFLZ	themselves THEPL/SAEFLZ	yourself KWROUR/SAEFL	yourselves KWROUR/SAEFLZ

Practical Exercise

☞ Practice the following until you can write them without hesitation:

John Jones had a compulsion to buy candy. He loved candy bars. He got a good deal from a man who / sold him 23,031 cartons of candy bars. He took them home and put them away.

His wife, Joan Jones, / had a compulsion for coffee. She loved to go to the market and buy coffee. She wanted to go to work / for a coffee company, but she didn't get the job. She had trouble because of her condition. She couldn't stop / buying coffee beans.

Jenny went out on a date with a policeman. They went out to have a meal but / had to be home soon because Jenny had to take an exam the next day. She had to study. While / they were out, the policeman wrote a ticket because her friend parked in a no parking zone. Her friend / became mad and tried not to pay the fine. Now, her friend is in jail.

Randy has an invention that / works like this: you say a word and a girl writes that word on a shorthand keyboard. The shorthand keyboard then takes / that word and puts it into a computer. The computer then writes the word on a screen. It is an / amazing invention. Randy has great vision to be able to make this great sensation.

Didn't he complete the transaction like / he was told to? 12 policemen came to his house. They put handcuffs on him and took him away. The / judge told him what his plea was. He said he didn't do it, and he ain't going to pay for / a crime he didn't do. It was like a script from a movie.

Fill out the application by noon. / Have your vision checked at once. Make sure that you have good diction. Don't forget your subtraction. What is your conviction? / What about addition? What will you do if you get a fraction? All policemen perform well when they have / too. I sent you a written notice about the mission. Please plan on arriving by 3 in the afternoon.

What / would you do if you had a chance to buy a house on a mountain for a very good price / and the day you had to move you had an important exam? Would you take the exam and pass the course, / or would you buy the house and fail the exam? What would you do?

How would you be able / to afford the house if you didn't pass the exam and got a good paying job? Your finances would not / allow you to buy the house. You couldn't pay your bills on time. How

33

about starting a repair shop for / shorthand keyboards? You could order materials for the keyboards and fix them in your basement. You could make a lot / of money if you were good at it.

Did you hear about the baby who fell in the tub / of soapy water and got all wet? She cried, but Rose saved her by pulling her out of the / tub and drying her off.

I began dancing all by myself. I then started running by myself. A friend / of mine was walking by herself. Then her friend joined her and they were talking to themselves.

Have you ever / had to go to a jury trial? There is a girl who is a juror in a case about a wreck between / a bus and an automobile. The man who was driving the bus got a lawyer who told him that he could / sue the girl who was driving the car. The girl who was driving the car got a lawyer who told / her she could sue the man who was driving the bus. Now, they are in court.

What a / collision it was. The complete motor dropped out of the bus. Then the motor fell into a hole in / the road and fell apart. Then the car ran over the motor and collided with a bike. What a complex / case. There was only 1 injury and that was to a dog, but the dog is beginning to feel better. /

Will you help organize a meeting of 38 people who belong to the company? They all manufacture shorthand keyboards / except for one girl who works with drapes. She makes drapes that are natural in color.

I will open the / case with a quote from the court. The court has ordered all people to stop talking about the case. If / the suit goes to court, you cannot talk about it. You can't give your legal opinion at all. You have to stop / this arguing about who will win the case. I hope you don't have to tell your story about the injury / because you can't.

Word Drill

☞ Review the following until you can write them without hesitation:

ditch TKEUFP	pitch PEUFP	witch WEUFP	stitch STEUFP
rich REUFP	glitch TKPWHREUFP	bunch PWUPB/AEFP	niche TPHEUFP
lunch HRUPB/AEFP	crunch KRUPB/AEFP	fish TPEURB	wish WEURB
dish TKEURB	mash PHARB	crash KRARB	cash KAERB
wash WARB	dash TKARB	stash STARB	racial RAEURBL
childish KHAOEULD/KWREURB	boyish PWOFPL/KWREURB	girlish TKPWEURL/KWREURB	babyish PWAEUB/KWREURB
spatial SPAEURBL	facial TPAEURBL	partial PAR/SHAEL	martial PHAR/SHAEL
delicious TKHREURBS	extra STRA	bonus PWOEPB/KWRUS	expression SKPREGS
ficticious TPEUBG/TEURBS	contentious KOPB/TEPB/SHAUS	shorthand SHORT/HAEPBD (1)	ice cream AOEUSZ/KRAOEPL
pernicious PER/NEURBS	frog TPROG	catch KAFP	sauce SAUS
saucy SAUS/AEFPL	zapped SKPWAPD	princess PREUPB/SES	charming KHARPLG
each AOEFP	inmate EUPB/PHAEUT	insane EUPB/SAEUPB	incur EUPB/KUR
incorrect EUPB/KREBGT	index EUPB/TKEFRPB	instill EUPB/STEUL	onset OPB/SET
ongoing OPB/TKPWOEG	enhance EPB/HAPBS	endure EPB/TKAOUR	ordeal OR/TKAOEL
enable EPB/KWRAEUBL	orchid OR/KEUD	orbit OR/PWEUT	ornate OR/TPHAEUT
organ OR/TKPWAPB	orchard OR/KHARD	pray PRAFPL	prance PRAPBS
precious PRERBS	press PRES	preach PRAOEFP	snow STPHOEFRP
snake STPHAEUBG	snap STPHAP	snag STPHAG	snail STPHAEUL
snug STPHUG	smart SPHART	smash SPHARB	smell SPHEL
smoke SPHOEBG	smog SPHOG	smear SPHAOER	caught KAUGT
snowballs (1) STPHOEFRP/PWAULZ	prairie PRAEUR/KWRAOE	throwing THROEFRPG	

(1) The AE stroke that joins the two words together is written in the word hand (HAEPBD). The word could also be written SHORT/AE/HAPBD.

☞ Review the following until you can write them without hesitation:

correspond KROPBD	credit KRE	customer KPHER	particular THRAR
peculiar KHRAR	photograph TPRAF	popular PHRAR	possible POB
prepare PRAOEP	principal PRAL	principle PR-L	probable PRAB
probably PRABL	problem PREPL	proceed PROE	always AULZ
all right HR-RT	until TPH-L	onto OPBT	machine PH-FP
practice PRA	present PREBPT	presence PREPBS	previous PR-FS
product PROBGT	program PRAPL	propose PR-P	profession PROFGS
type TAOEUP	provide PROEU	approximate PRAFRPB	appropriate PROEPT
church KH-FP	special SP-RB	specially SP-RBL	

Miscellaneous Drill

☞ Review the following until you can write them without hesitation:

I'm AOEUPLZ	they're THERZ	we're WERZ
you're URZ	open quote KWO-RBGS	end quote KWE-RBGS
surround quotes SKW-RBGS	$5.97 5/DZ/7EU9/SZ	$59.23 59/DZ/23/SZ
$111.77 1/HPBD/1EU/DZ/EU7/SZ	$9,456.72 9/THZ/4/HPBD/56/DZ/2EU7/SZ	$1,567,982.60 1/PHL/5/HPBD/67/THZ/9/HPBD/2EU8/DZ/0EU6/SZ

Practical Exercise

☞ Practice the following until you can write them without hesitation:

What a sensation (SEPB/SAEUGS). What an amazement: People who can write words on a shorthand machine at about 300 words a minute. / Can you write like that? I can't. I can only go about 225.

I got a bill from my doctor / for $945,882.54. I paid the bill but there has to be a mistake. Payment was put in the mail; / I paid by check. My check number is 44590. I will double check to see if I sent it / to the right address (A/TKRES).

The document I have says that there is a job open for men and women who / like to cook. It pays about $6.75 an hour for a year (KWRAOER), then it pays over $10 an / hour. I will apply for the job, but I need an application. Can you get me one? I need employment, / and I need it now. My bills are so high they reach the sky.

My particular goal is to get / a job. If I can earn about $500 a week, I will be all right. It would / be better if I could make $1000 a week, but I will be happy with a fraction of / that. Half of it would help out.

I will make an arrangement with you. I will give you half of / what I earn if you tell me where to put my money so that it will grow. I need to put / aside about $467.87 a week to pay for my new automobile. It is sleek. It is sharp. It is a / Porsche (POR/AERB).

What an insane thought. He wants to go to the prairie to ski (SKAOE). He says that there is a snow / storm due (TKAOU) there any day now. I will bet you it won't snow until next year.

The index shows / that no snow is expected (SKPEBGT/AED) until a week or 2. My profession is telling people what to do. I love / to tell them where to go. Some people can't endure. Some people make a big ordeal about it. / Will you enroll (EPB/ROEL) in the program now?

A snail and a snake had a race. I will tell / you who won the race if you give me a cookie (KAOBG/KWRAOE). Janet picked a red orchid from the orchard / and gave it to her boy friend. He gave her a watch (WAFP). Now, they are happy.

Joe says, "How now brown / cow." Jill says, "The rain in Spain stays on the plane." I say, "Sun is fun when you're on the / run." I propose to give you $78.92 to pay for the rug. You would be smart to buy one / at that price. You can't go wrong. It is a fine rug that I hope to put in my / new diner. I will give you dinner in my diner.

He found a precious stone in the grass. He sold / the stone for $78,390 and then bought (PWOUGT) stock. His stock split; and, now, he has $987,456. He can't / spend all the money he has. Wouldn't you save some money? I would. My mom always used to say, "Save for / a rainy day." Now, it is raining and I have no money.

There was an inmate named Ben; his / real name was Stan. He stole (STOEL) $567,987.32 from the principal of the school. The principal caught him in / the act. He said: "I didn't do it. I ain't the one. You got the wrong guy." He says his friend / Tom did it. Tom says he's insane. I saw the crime and it was Fred who did it. Now, Fred / says he didn't. What a complex plot this is. It was a movie all the time.

My / cat's name is quagmire (KWAG/PHAOEUR). We call her "kitty" (KEUT/AEFPL) for short. She loves to bring home gifts (TKPWEUFTS) for us. She brought (PWROUGT) / home a bat, a rat, and a snake all in one day. She was so proud.

Word Drill

☞ Review the following until you can write them without hesitation:

arson AR/SOPB	wagon WAG/KWROPB	cannon KAPB/KWROPB
lemon HREPL/KWROPB	mason PHAEU/SOPB	melon PHEL/KWROPB
baton PWA/TOPB	nylon TPHFPL/HROPB	salon SA/HROPB
eaten AOET/KWREPB	olden OELD/KWREPB	liken HRAOEUBG/KWREPB
risen REUZ/KWREPB	linen HREUPB/KWREPB	waken WAEUBG/KWREPB
widen WAOEUD/KWREPB	actor ABGT/KWROR	armor ARPL/KWROR
error ER/KWROR	honor HOPB/KWROR	humor HAOUPL/KWROR
minor PHAOEUPB/KWROR	razor RAEUZ/KWROR	tutor TAOUT/KWROR
vigor SREUG/KWROR	alter ALT/KWRER	buyer PWUFPL/KWRER
anger APBG/KWRER	dinner TKEUPB/KWER	diner TKAOEUPB/KWRER
eager AOEG/KWRER	fewer TPEFRP/KWRER	older OELD/KWRER
finer TPAOEUPB/KWRER	prepaid PRE/PAEUD	premier PRE/PHAOER
predate PRE/TKAEUT	predict PRE/TKEUBGT	prevent PRE/SREPBT
promote PRO/PHOET	prorate PRO/RAEUT	protect PRO/TEBGT
proportion PRO/PORGS	remit RE/PHEUT	resume RE/SKPWAOUPL
recall RE/KAUL		resent RE/SKPWEPBT
revoke RE/SROEBG	destroy TKE/STROFPL	deliver TKHREUFR
depart TKPART	demand TKPHAPBD	removed RE/PHOFBD
bookcase PWAOBG/KAES	license HRAOEUS/KWREPBS	paper PAEUP/KWRER
wanted WAPBT/AED	attend A/TEPBD	mistake PHEUS/TAE
winter WEUPBT/KWRER	attraction A/TRABGS	4-wheel 4/H-RBGS/WHAOEL
mentioned PHEPBGS/AED	proceeds PRO/SAOEDZ	signs SAOEUPBZ
recount RE/KOUPBT	squeeze SKWAOEZ	squeezed SKWAOEZ/AED
alley AL/AEFPL	eggs EGZ	bargain PWAR/TKPWAEUPB

Short Form Drill

☞ Review the following until you can write them without hesitation:

occur KUR	office TPEUS	obtain OBT	today TOD
tomorrow TOR	yesterday KWRAFPL	report RORT	remember RER
remind REUPBD	return RURPB	request RELGTS	represent REPT
worry WOER	woman WAPB	women WEPB	wherever WHREFR
whenever WHEFR	volunteer SRO	volume SROUPL	visible SREUBL
victim SREUBGT	upon POPB	unless TPH-LS	unwilling TPH-FRP
notice TPH-TS	recent RAOEPBT		

☞ Review the following until you can write them without hesitation:

I'd AOEUDZ	he'd HAEDZ	she'd SHAEDZ	they'd THEDZ
we'd WAEDZ	you'd UDZ	open paren PRO-RBGS	close paren PRE-RBGS

background PWABG/AE/TKPWROUPBD	outlay OUT/AE/HRAFPL
stairway STAEUR/WAEFPL	driveway TKRAOEUFB/WAEFPL
self-imposed SEFL/H-RBGS/EUPL/POEZ/AED	bi-lateral PWEU/H-RBGS/HRAT/RAL
pro-life PRO/H-RBGS/LAOEUF	letter-by-letter spelling A-FL, PW-FL, KR-FL...

☞ Practice the following until you can write them without hesitation:

There was a farmer (TPARPL/KWRER) who sold eggs for a living. He sold them by the basket (PWAS/KET). A big basket of eggs was / $56.92 while a small basket of eggs was $34.24. If you buy three big baskets of eggs, he / will give you one small basket free if you donate (TKOE/TPHAEUT) some of the eggs to the church.

A woman and / a man robbed a store at gunpoint (TKPWUPB/AE/POEUPBT). They got away with over $5,000. The police are looking for them / right now. If you see them, will you call a policeman? They'd come right away. They might give you a reward (RE/WARD) / if you help find the robbers (ROB/KWRERZ).

Jim didn't want to do his homework (HOEPL/AE/WORBG). He couldn't do addition or subtraction. He hates / fractions. Will you help him?

John made lemon juice (SKWRAOUS); Jill made melon juice. They made it all by themselves. It / was bad. They gave it to their dog, and their dog got sick. They gave it to their cat, and their / cat ran away. They fed some to their plants, and their plants grew taller.

If you will complete the transaction, / you will be a rich man. If you don't, you will be poor. The tension in here is great. Can't / you feel the tension in the air? Please pass the salt (SAULT) and pepper (PEP/KWRER) now.

Any proceeds from the sale of / the books will go to the school. The proportion that they will get may be great or it may be small. / I predict they will make about $75,000 if they sell enough books. Do they have that many?

The man / said: "My name is Ed, and I lived in Denver." I thought he said his name was Fred. Then he / spelled his name for me. He spelled it T-E-D. Now, I'm sure his name is not Ed/ or Fred, but it is Ted.

A horse who could walk on a rope was the premier attraction at the / show. The horse fell on a crowd of people. If I depart now, I can be home by noon. I / will resume my place at the table when I arrive. I should be home by winter; if not, call the / police. If the snow gets too deep, I will call a snowplow (STPHOEFRP/AE/PHROFRP)..

He said he would deliver the equipment / today, but he made an error. I won't get the material until tomorrow. I had to call in a volunteer / to help put it away. He hurt his hand when he smashed it in the door. Now, he can't work / for me; and I'll have to call my boss.

She'd study if she could. He'd study if he could. They'd / study if they should. I'd deliver the paper to the red house, but there is a big brown dog on / the porch (POR/AEFP). I'm afraid of dogs who bark and growl (TKPWROFRPL). I am an unwilling victim. I can't let a dog / destroy the paper or my job. I resent having to run away from the dog. I'll call the police, and / they can take care of him.

I gave the man $98.23 to take care of the cats in my / basement. I had 892 cats. I didn't want them there. The man came and took them away. / Now, I have no cats; but I have 3,452 mice (PHAOEUS).

There was a collision. The manager ran away. I / have a new motor for my car. The engine runs great. The jury said, "yes," when they should have / said, "no." My cat is a great comfort to me. My dog is also. 6 days ago a cow ran / away with a horse. They have not been seen since. They got themselves in a lot of trouble. They are / wanted by the police.

If I practice now, I won't have to practice later (HRAEUT/KWRER). I have a special request. Please / remind your friends to give money to me. I need it to pay my bills. They can send me / money at my home address (A/DRES). I'll be home until 9 tomorrow, then I have to go to jail.

I want to / win a prize. I have to sell 17,000 tickets by tomorrow afternoon. Will you buy 1,000 tickets from me? / If you do, I'll add 6 yams for you to cook. I made an error. I only have to sell / 15,000 tickets, but I need to have the money by today. Will you buy 5,000 tickets? If you / do, I'll give you a free pen.

My dad and mom belong to a club where they get dressed up / in armor and have a war. They shoot a cannon into the night sky. Fewer and fewer people go out at / night when the sky is full of noise (TPHOEUZ) from a cannon.

I'm glad that the actor was only acting when he / said, "Get out of here or you'll get yours." I thought he was talking to me. My television (TEL/SREUGS) was too / loud. I'm glad I have a sense of humor, and I can laugh at myself.

Jen kissed a frog, / and it turned into a prince. Jeff kissed a frog, and it turned into a princess (PREUPB/SES). I kissed a frog, / and it turned into a snake. I wish I had a dish of fish to pass. I'd love to put sauce / on my fish in the dish.

A customer came into the store and said he wanted a double fish and / chips to go. I gave it to him, and he paid me with a $50.00 bill. Then he said, "Keep / the money for a tip." I was glad because the fish and chips was only $5.00. That means / my tip was $45.00. Now, I can buy my own dish of fish and chips.

I won / first prize for the photograph I took of a bird in a bush (PWURB). It was great. My prize was a / whole year's (YAOER/AOS) subscription (SUB/SKREUPGS) to the photograph journal (SKWRAOURPBL).

My mom is peculiar. She makes lunch out of jelly and bread. / My dad is peculiar; he takes it to work and eats it. He loves jelly. I can tell because / when he comes home from work, he has it all over his face. I love ice cream. I would / probably have 22 ice cream cones (KOEPBZ) in a day if I could. The problem is, I can't. I can't / because I don't have the money or the credit. I won't because I don't want to get sick. /

Word Drill

☞ Review the following until you can write them without hesitation:

surely SHAOURL	safely SAEUFL	
lately HRAEUT/HRAEFPL	sadly SAD/HRAEFPL	badly PWAD/HRAEFPL
rarely RAEURL	lonely HROEPBL	timely TAOEUPL/HRAEFPL
scarcely SKAEURS/HRAEFPL	wisely WAOEUZ/HRAEFPL	likely HRAOEUBG/HRAEFPL
daily TKAEUL/AEFPL	early ERL/AEFPL	jelly SKWREL/AEFPL
trouble TROUBL	stubble STUBL	double TKOUBL
bubble PWUBL	ample APL/PAEL	sample SAPL/PAEL
apple AP/AEL	maple PHAUP/AEL	rubble RUBL
angle APBG/AEL	waffle WAFL	hassle HAS/AEL
tassel TAS/KWREL	offer OFR	over OEFR
cover KOFR	never TPHEFR	sliver SHREUFR
silver SEUL/SRER	wafer WAFR	waiver WAEUFR
waver WAEFR	suffer SUFR	safer SAFR
saver SAEUFR	extra STRA	exile SKPAOEUL
expel SKPEL	excellent SKPHREPBT	extol STOL
exhume SKPAOUPL	excise SKPAOEUZ	exhale SKPHAEUL
exact SKPABGT	excuse SKPAOUS	excuse SKPAOUZ
exam SKPAPL	excite SKPAOEUT	execute SKPAOUT
express SKPRES	excess SKPES	excellence SKPHREPBS
exercise SKPER/SAOEUZ	expedite SKPE/TKAOEUT	two TWO
twin TWEUPB	twilight TWEU/HRAOEUGT	twirl TWEURL
tweed TWAOED	twice TWAOEUS	trench TREPB/AEFP
trap TRAP	trip TREUP	train TRAEUPB
trolley TROL/AEFPL	trumpet TRUPL/PET	

Short Form Drill

☞ Review the following until you can write them without hesitation:

ability ABLT	above PWOFB	accept SEP	ask SK-
basis PWEUS	certain SERPB	certificate SERT	department TKEPT
difference TPREPBS	different TPREPBT	dozen TKOZ	easy AOES
x-ray SKPRAFPL	excel SKP-L	notice TPH-TS	develop TKEFL
difficult TKEUFT	effect EFBGT	effort EFRT	familiar TPHRAR
gallon TKPW-L	finish TP-RB	accident STK-PBT	husband HUZ
really R-L	truly T-FPL		

Miscellaneous Drill

☞ Review the following until you can write them without hesitation:

I've AOEUFZ	they've THEFZ	we've WEFZ	you've UFZ
exclamation point (!) SKP-RBGS	slash (/) SHR-RBGS	9:47 a.m. K9/47/APL	4:22 p.m. 4BG/2EU/P-PL
12 o'clock 12/AOBG	5 o'clock 5/AOBG	4:49 p.m. 4BG/49/P-PL	1400 hours 14/HPBD/HOURZ

9/7/49 9/SHR-RBGS/7/SHR-RBGS/49	10-29-50 10/H-RBGS/20/H-RBGS/50
11/30/94 1EU/SHR-RBGS/30/SHR-RBGS/4EU9	12-24-81 12/H-RBGS/24/H-RBGS/1EU8

Practical Exercise

☞ Practice the following:

Did you hear what effect lack of sleep has on your brain? They say that the less sleep you have, / the more mistakes you make. They say that you need a minimum of 6 to 8 hours of sleep a night, / but this is not always possible. If you lose sleep one night, you must make it up at some/ time.

Meg had a choice between two skirts. She could have chosen (KHOEZ/KWREPB) a tan tweed or a red plaid (PLAD). She didn't / like the tweed in tan or the plaid in red, so she chose a red tweed.

Does Jim play the trumpet? / We are looking for a man or woman who can play it for our school band. We already have people / who play drums and flutes; all we need now is a trumpeter (TRUPL/PET/KWRER).

I went to the store to get a lemon. / They were all out of lemons so I had to settle (SET/AEL) for a melon. I brought (BROUGT) the melon home, but / it was rotten. Have you ever had a rotten melon? It was very, very bad.

Peg had to perform at / 6, but she didn't get home until 5:30 p.m. She had to scurry (SKUR/AEFPL) around the house in order / to be ready by 5:45. Her dad was going to take her to the hall, but he had an / accident on the way. Her mom had to take her. By the time she got to the hall, it was / packed; and she didn't have time to practice. Her twin, Meg, was already there. Peg and Meg performed very / well for the crowd. One of the girls twirls a baton while one toots (TAOTS) a horn. What a great show. / They won first prize.

You are hereby (HAOERB) given notice that you are to report to Doctor Jones's (SKWROEPBZ/AOS) office at / 12 o'clock sharp. You have an appointment to have an x-ray taken of your head. He will take no excuse; you better / be there on time, or he will cancel (KAPBS/KWREL) all appointments.

Have you ever gone skiing in the twilight? What a thrill. / You can't see your hand in front of your face. It's like skiing in the dark. I tried it yesterday, / and I fell in a ditch. I didn't get hurt, but I smashed my skis to bits. Now, I can't / ski until next winter when I'll buy a new pair of skis.

A train ticket will set you back about / $100 unless you buy the super (SPER) special which only will be $99.99, but you have to buy it / today by 7 o'clock. The train leaves at 7:22, so be on time. If you miss the train, take / the trolley. You can ride the trolley for $10.52, but it will take you 8 hours to get to where / you are going. The train is twice as quick, but ten times the price. Which one will you choose?

Please / make an extra effort to finish by 9:05 p.m. We plan to study at 9:15, and we need the / table. I want you out of here by exactly 9:14, or I'll get very mad. You've got a right / to demand what you want to do because you own the house. We're all here to help you stand up / for your rights. We've been through this before. John said, "Now is the time that we all stand side by / side."

I'll ask you one more time: Do you want to take the exam at 9 o'clock in the morning or / 4 o'clock in the afternoon? If you don't want to tell me right now, that's all right. I can arrange / to have to take it at 7:22 a.m. or 6:15 p.m.

Bart (PWART) looked sadly because his / dog ran away. He used to treat his dog badly. He would not feed it for days. I can't / blame the dog for running away. His dog's name was Rover (ROEFR). Have you seen Rover? If you do, give / a whistle (WHEUS/AEL) and he will come running to you. If you find him, take him to Bart. Bart said he will / never treat Rover wrongly again. Bart loves Rover.

If I had a dozen eggs, I'd cook them. The only / problem is, John wants me to fry them and Joan wants me to scramble (SKRAPL/BAEL) them. I want them sunny-side / up. My little boy, Tom, who is only 4, wants me to color them red for his basket.

You can / scarcely see the difference between night and day at twilight. There is really a fine line between dark and light. / It is only a fraction of a minute between day and night, dark and light. Some say that night is / different than day because of the amount of light you don't see. Some say the difference is in the amount / of light you do see. What do you say? What difference does it make?

John is in deep, deep trouble. / John is in double trouble. He was going to pick up his mom and take her to the store / and then to lunch, but he forgot. He went to get ice cream instead (EUPB/STED). He got a maple cone. His mom / was mad. What would you do if you were his mom? John did take her an ice cream cone, / and that made her feel better.

Please go to the shorthand department and pick up a waiver for the next / exam. Without the certificate, you will have to take the exam. Are you ready or not? Surely, you can't be / ready after only 15 minutes of practice. It requires about 9 hours of practice. It is my opinion that you / will pass the exam with flying colors if you practice 10 hours; you'll fail the exam if you don't. Good / luck.

UNIT 8
DRILL XVI (Lessons 31-32)

Word Drill

☞ Review the following until you can write them without hesitation:

safety SAEUFT	clarity KHRAEURT	charity KHAEURT
brevity PWREFT	density TKEPBS/TAEFPL	humidity HAOUPLD/TAEFPL
minority PHAOEU/TPHORT	majority PHAPBLGT	sensitivity SEPBS/TEUFT
tranquillity TRAPB/KWEULT	booty PWAOT/AEFPL	rarity RAEURT
nerve TPHEFRB	serve SEFRB	swerve SWEFRB
surf SUFRB	turf TUFRB	dwarf TKWAFRB
curve KUFRB	starve STAFRB	carve KAFRB
scarf SKAFRB	knew STPEFRP	new TPHEFRP
knot STPOT	not TPHOT	knight STPAOEUGT
night TPHAOEUGT	knead STPAOED	need TPHAOED
knee STPAOE	kneel STPAOEL	know STPOEFRP
known STPOEPB	knot STPOT	knock STPOBG
knife STPAOEUF	knit STPEUT	knuckle STPUBG/AEL
knapsack STPAP/AE/SABG	spree SPRAOE	spray SPRAFPL
sprite SPRAOEUT	sprig SPREUG	sprint SPREUPBT
spirit SPEURT	spurt SPURT	strut STRUT
strike STRAOEUBG	stroll STROEL	strip STREUP
stripe STRAOEUP		

Short Form Drill

☞ Review the following until you can write them without hesitation:

service S-FB	wonderful WOFL	whatever WHAFR	usual AOURB
unusual TPHAOURB	usually AOURBL	unusually TPHAOURBL	technical T-FP
support SUPT	sudden SUD	supervise SPR-FB	sufficient SUF
suggest SUG	incident STKEUPBT	accomplish PHREURB	account K-PBT
data TKAT	daughter TKAUR	deduct TK-BGT	suppose SPOEZ

Miscellaneous Drill

☞ Review the following until you can write them without hesitation:

I'll AOEUFRPZ	it'll T-FRPZ	he'll HAEFRPZ	she'll SHAEFRPZ
they'll THEFRPZ	we'll WEFRPZ	you'll UFRPZ	hyphen (-) H-RBGS
back slash (\) PW-RBGS	dash (--) TK-RBGS	A. B. ... A-FPD, PW-FPD ...	

Practical Exercise

☞ Practice the following:

I have a friend who lives out of his knapsack. He keeps the following in there: his lunch, / a jar of jelly, a bowl of rice, 11 books for class, 6 spare shirts, a pair (PAEUR) of jeans (SKWRAOEPBZ), 1 / sneaker (STPHAOEBG/KWRER), a beeper (PWAOEP/KWRER), a clock that doesn't keep time, a Mickey Mouse watch, his pet frog, 4 cats, a mouse, a / computer, 1 pen, a pack of paper, and 42 marbles. His knapsack is his life. He doesn't go any place / without (WOUT) it.

My account at the bookstore (PWAOBG/AE/STOR) is overdue (OEFR/DAOU). I now owe $456,981.41. How did it get / so high? Probably because I gave my friends my credit card and they went wild. Now, I don't know what / to do. I'm worried (WOERD) that they will send the police to my room and take me to jail. I called / my mom and dad, but they weren't home. Will you help me? Lend me $500,000, and I'll pay you / back tomorrow. You can even deduct a small fee if you'd like.

Did you see the knight knock down the / man? He broke his knuckle and then his knee. I knew the knight was tough, but I didn't know / he was that rough. I'm going to call the police if he doesn't leave the man alone. He is / having a difficult time.

Can you sprint? I cannot. Can you spurt? I can't. Do you have any spirit? I / don't. Are you ready to go? I'm not. Can you strut? Not me. Have you ever collected data? I have, but / I didn't do it right; it was all wrong. I can't even account for my own record.

There was an / accident on the corner (KORPB/KWRER) of Maple and Main at 5:13 a.m. A man in an automobile ran into a / store that was baking fresh bread. The car ran into the oven on the left side and came out on / the right side with 12 dozen loaves (HROEFBZ) of freshly baked bread in the front seat. The man was lucky because / he was hungry (HUPBG/RAEFPL). He drove around the block and went through again and asked for some jelly. This time the / police were waiting for him. His greed for jelly got him in trouble. Now, he is in jail where he / can have all the bread and jelly he wants.

Here is a recipe (RES/PAOE) for a most delicious cookie: knead some dough, / add salt, water, 12 eggs, and some sour cream. Mix it in a bowl (PWOEFRPL) until it is thick. Put it in / a pan and cook it for 20 minutes at 450. When they turn brown, you'll know they're done. Take / them out of the oven and eat them before they're all gone.

47

I'm not supposed to eat any cookies because / my doctor told me so. He smelled my freshly baked cookies and knocked at my door. He demanded that I / give him every cookie I made. I did, except for the six dozen I put away in the cookie / jar. He came back ten minutes later and found me eating the stash. By the time he came back, / I'd eaten 25 of them. I don't feel so good.

Can you knit? I can. I knit a pair of / mittens (PHEUT/KWREPBZ) for my precious little cat. My cat's name is mittens. I knit mittens for mittens. I know my cat / loves them, because she won't go out of the house unless I put them on her little feet. I had / to knit two pair because she has 4 feet. I knit one pair in black and one pair in white. /

Please report the incident to the police right away. They will want to know the following: Who did it? What / time did it happen? Where were you when it happened? Were you alone when it happened? Why did it happen? / Can you give them the data they need? If you don't know, tell them so. Don't lie because / they'll find out and you'll be in trouble.

If you support a charity, pick one that is a good / cause (KAUZ). You'll be smart to look into it before you send any money. A good charity is one that helps fight / abuse and sickness. They say, "Every penny you send helps save a life."

My slogan (SLOEG/KWRAPB) is this: "Never give / up." Even if I feel like giving up, I don't. I never waver from my saying. I never swerve. I / keep on trying. I tried yesterday, I'm trying today, and I'll try even harder tomorrow.

Did you hear that crash? / It sounded like a big truck skidded around a curve. Maybe it hit the curb. Let's go see what happened. Before / we go, we better call the police so they can come and take a look. I hope there wasn't an / accident.

My dad used to say: "The price of tranquility is peace (PAOESZ) of mind." Now, I know what he meant (PHEPBT). My mom / used to say: "The price you pay for peace of mind is very little, all you need to do is / look within (W-PB) your heart" (HAERT). Now, I know what she meant.

John had the nerve to call me up at 4:17 / a.m. and wake (WAEBG) me up out of a sound sleep. I was dreaming about taking down dictation (TKEUBG/TAEUGS) at 225 / words per minute. I was getting every single (SEUPBG/AEL) word the teacher said. I was amazing. Now that John woke me / up, I'll probably never get to that speed again in my life. He wanted to know if I was asleep. /

I can provide the following service for a small fee: I can clean your machine for $55.92, / I can change your ribbon (REUB/KWROPB) for $23.98, I can oil the clutch for $21.18, or I can clean / the case and put in a new tray for only $4.54. I have a special this month--all / of the above for $100 flat. I suggest you take the special service at the special price. It's a / great deal.

What does the majority say? What does the minority say? Do you have any sensitivity? Do you speak / with clarity? What kind of technical support do they offer? Will there always be someone there to help you?

Would / you prefer the surf and turf or the fish and chips? I'd prefer the surf and fish to the turf / and chips. The waiter (WAEUT/KWRER) said they were out of surf and chips so I ended (EPBD/AED) up with fish and turf. / I didn't mind the fish, it was delicious, but the turf was terrible (TAEURBL). It reminded me of mud soup (SOUP) we used / to make as little boys and girls. I didn't mind it until the waiter brought the bill; it was for / $571.12. I fainted and never woke up until the next morning. I woke up in jail.

I'll have an / unusual meal this afternoon. I'll mix apple and maple and make a thick jelly. Then I'll put it in a / pie and bake it in an oven and see what it looks like. If it is delicious, I'll sell it / as maple-apple surprise (SUR/PRAOEUZ). What an unusual sounding dessert. Want to try some? It's really not that unusual; in fact, / the dinner down the street usually serves (SEFRBZ) it every day at noon.

UNIT 9
DRILL XVII (Lessons 33-34)

Word Drill

☞ Review the following until you can write them without hesitation:

adorable A/TKORBL	deplorable TKE/PHRORBL
assessable A/SES/KWRABL	regrettable RE/TKPWRET/KWRABL
durable TKAOURBL	dependable TKPEPBD/KWRABL
compatible KPAT/KWREUBL	commendable KPHEPBD/KWRABL
accessible AK/SES/KWREUBL	comfortable K-FRT/KWRABL
sensible SEPBS/KWREUBL	compatability KPAT/KWRABLT
durability TKAOURBLT	accessibility AK/SES/KWREUBLT
sensibility SEPBS/KWREUBLT	dependability TKPEPBD/KWRABLT
entertain EPBT/TAEUPB	enterprise EPBT/PRAOEUZ
intersection EUPBT/SEBGS	intercede EUPBT/SAOED
interpose EUBPT/POEZ	interface EUPBT/TPAEUS
interrupt EUPBT/RUPT	intersession EUPBT/SEGS
dispel STKPEL	disprove STKPROFB
disable STKAEUBL	design STKAOEUPB
disallow STKA/HROFRP	disassociate STKA/SOERBT
despair STKPAEUR	disservice TKEUS/S-FB
disparity STKPAEURT	disclaimer TKEUS/KHRAEUPL/KWRER

Short Form Drill

☞ Review the following until you can write them without hesitation:

America PHERBG	hospital HOPT	human HAOUPL
amount APLT	American PHERPB	hotel HOELT
article ARL	advance SRAPBS	motel PHOELT
against TKPWEPBS	avenue AFB	auto AUT
disclose STKHROEZ	destroy STKROFPL	discuss STKUS
distribute STKREUBT	discussion STKUGS	discount STKOUPBT
distribution STKREUBGS	distinguish STKWEURB	disagree STKRAOE
especial SPERB	especially SPERBL	

50

☞ Review the following until you can write them without hesitation:

how's HOFRPZ	it's T-Z	that's THAZ
there's THRZ	what's WHAZ	where's WHRZ
who's WHOZ	decimal point TKP-RBGS	point POEU-RBGS
Monday PHO-FPLT	Tuesday TU-FPLT	Wednesday WE-FPLT
Thursday THU-FPLT	Friday TPREU-FPLT	Saturday SA-FPLT
Sunday SU-FPLT	one half WUPB/HAF	two thirds TWO/THEURDZ
1/2 1R/2	2/3 2R/3	3/4 3R/4
8/10 R8/10	6/7 R6/7	9/10 R9/10

Practical Exercise

☞ Practice the following:

Can you tell me if the service is on Tuesday or Thursday night? I know it was one of the nights / that begin with the letter "T," but I can't remember which one it was. Maybe it was Saturday or Sunday. / Will you call the office for me and let me know. It is a very special meeting that I don't want / to miss. I'll bet all of the people in the class are doctors, lawyers, or teachers. The class will teach / us how to use a computer to do what we want it to do.

It is a very sensible / class. The amount of money that I have to pay is only $45.34 for the first 7 classes. After that, / if I want to, I can pay only $495 for the entire (EPB/TAOEUR) year. I know that's a real bargain, / don't you? I paid $239.82 in advance so now I only owe $15.92 per month for 23 / months. I can't even buy a new auto for that price!

I feel very comfortable about buying a new house / on credit. It is adorable. It has a white fence around the back yard and a big maple tree in / the front yard. I took out a loan for $458,981.32 to pay for the house, but I know / I can afford it. My weekly paycheck (PAFPL/AE/KHEBG) is $1,902.91. My job as a court reporter pays / well. I'm going to have a new in-ground swimming pool put in and a spa and a three-car / garage for my Cadillac, my Porsche, and my Rambler (RAPL/PWHRER). Some people say I'm a dreamer. What / do you say?

How dependable are you? It is regrettable that you can't be here for the party. I heard / that you broke your leg on a skiing trip. Are you walking with crutches yet? If so, are you / finding most houses are accessible?

When I went away for a workshop on how to be a court reporter I / stayed in a hotel called the Americana (PHERPB/TPHA). It was a nice place, except for the food. The food was terrible / (TAEURBL). All they served was exotic (SKPOT/KWREUBG) stuff. I ordered a burnt burger and greasy (TKPWRAOES/AEFPL) fries, and you should see what / they brought me. I can't even pronounce the name because it was French (TPREPB/AEFP). I couldn't eat it, so I / asked for a doggie (TKOG/KWRAOE) bag and took it home /to my cat, Steno.

What's this I hear about who's been taking you know whom (WHOPL) to you know where? Now, / where's the place that they will be seen next? I know. They're going to a show. How / do I know? A little bird told me so!

Monday is the day I do the shopping. Tuesday is the day / I do the laundry (HRAUPBD/RAEFPL). Wednesday is the day I do the cleaning. Thursday is the day I iron (AOEURPB). Friday I / usually go out to diner and a movie with my friend. Saturday I play, and Sunday I go to / church and then relax (RE/HRAFRPB). I also practice every day, usually at 6 o'clock in the morning because then I can practice / by myself.

The interest on the loan was 9.23. My old interest rate was 10.32. I know I / have a better interest rate at this bank; what do you have? If I can save about $12.03 a / week, I'll be richer than I was before.

Did you know that 2/3 of every 1/3 of every / dollar that is saved in America goes to feed the poor. What a great human effort; to feed the hungry / (HUPBG/RAEFPL). What a difficult enterprise to undertake, but I know it can be done without any more discussion. If we're / going to do it, let's do it. We'd better get started today, not tomorrow.

Please practice the words disallow, / discussion, disassociate, despair, and design, so that you can write them quickly and comfortably. Compatibility is the key.

Do not / interpose any new design at this point. It is way too late. It'll only add to the / confusion (KOPB/TPAOUGS), if you do. We have enough to discuss. I'm referring to the fact that a new interface design at this point / would be definitely desirable; but, can we afford it? The new design will be number 445-238-MQT-28.

UNIT 9
DRILL XVIII (Lessons 35-36)

Word Drill

☞ Review the following until you can write them without hesitation:

sang SAPBG	sank SAFBG	bang PWAPBG
bank PWAFBG	rang RAPBG	rank RAFBG
thing THEUPBG	think THEUFBG	sing SEUPBG
sink SEUFBG	ding TKEUPBG	tank TAFBG
tinge TEUFPBLG	range RAFPBLG	binge PWEUFPBLG
singe SEUFPBLG	fringe TPREUFPBLG	forbid TPOER/PWEUD
forgot TPOER/TKPWOT	forego TPOER/TKPWOE	forward TPOER/WARD
foreword TPOER/WORD	foretell TPOER/TEL	forget TPOER/TKPWET
forgive TPOER/TKPWEUFB	forgiven TPOER/TKPWEUFPB	forgave TPOER/TKPWAEUFB
uncover UPB/KOFR	unable UPB/KWRAEUBL	unnecessary UPB/TPHE
unclear UPB/KHRAOER	un-cola UPB/H-RBGS/KOE/HRA	unforgettable UPB/FOER/TKPWET/KWRABL
divorce TKWORS	divide TKWAOEUD	division TKWEUGS
devise TKWAOEUZ	devote TKWOET	devotion TKWOEGS
device TKWAOEUS	diverse TKWERS	devine TKWAOEUPB
devour TKWOUR	deviate TKWAEUT	deviation TKWAEUGS

Short Form Drill

☞ Review the following until you can write them without hesitation:

advertise TEUZ	advice SREUS	advise SREUZ	affect AFBGT
confer KER	connect KEBGT	connection KEBGS	conference KERPBS
consider KR-	considerable KR-B	considerably KR-BL	considerate KR-T
inch TPH-FP	include KHRAU	incorporate TPHORPT	incorporated TPHORPD
increase TPHRAOES	indicate KAET	beyond KWROPBD	used AOUDZ
authority THORT	capital KAL	orange ORPBG	continue T-PB

53

☞ Review the following until you can write them without hesitation:

Ray KEU-RBGS/RAFPL	(A) A-FPS
Joy KEU-RBGS/SKWROFPL	(H) H-FPS
Mark KEU-RBGS/PHARBG	(N) TPH-FPS
Frank KEU-RBGS/TPRAFBG	(V) SR-FPS
Matt KEU-RBGS/PHAT	(W) W-FPS
Rose KEU-RBGS/ROEZ	(X) SKP-FPS
OUT KA-RBGS/OUT	(Y) KWR-FPS
NOW KA-RBGS/TPHOFRP	(Z) SKPW-FPS

Practical Exercise

☞ Practice the following:

Fay sang a sad song badly, or was it a bad song sadly? He tried to sing it while a / friend played the drum. It was horrible (HORBL). Our dog wouldn't even stay in the same house. She left in a / hurry and ran out the door. I hope they take my advice and practice before they sing again. They are / supposed to be in a show tomorrow, but I don't think they are ready.

Will you buy my orange / Ford? It'll save you lots of money in gas. It gets 22 miles to the gallon on the highway and / 28 miles to the gallon around town. It only has 200 miles on it because it's brand new. / I have to sell it because my bill for school came today!

Mark and Frank were in the choir (KWOEUR). They / sang songs in front of a crowd. Mark sang solo (SO/HROE) because Frank sang so (SOE) low (HROEFRP) you couldn't hear him. /

Do you know the different ways of writing these words: rang and range and rank? If you do, you're smart. / Can you write them quickly? How about sang and sank? How about think and thing? How about knew and new or not / and knot? You're getting better every day.

I suppose you think this new way of writing is quite difficult. Well, / it's not. It's really quite easy. All you have to do is practice. However, consider this: 1/3 of all / people who learn how to write shorthand never use it. They don't want to. 1/3 of the 2/3 / remaining use it sparingly (SPAEURG/HRAEFPL). The remaining 1/3 use it every day and are very happy.

You must divorce yourself / from all bad habits when you practice. You can't practice in a noisy room. You shouldn't practice while watching / TV. You must practice with complete concentration (KOPBS/TRAEUGS). And you must read back considerably. Also, transcribe as much as you can. / You might have some fun if you devise a plan for practicing at the same time every day. I knew / a man who used to get up at 6 o'clock in the morning and practice for one and a / half hours before he went to work. When he came home, he would practice for 3/4 of an hour before / he went to bed.

I know a man and a woman who started their own freelance (TPRAOE/HRAEPBS) court reporting company. / It is called Steno and Steno, Incorporated. They do a lot of work for lawyers in the town. Yesterday / they had 12 jobs each. Today they each have 6. Tomorrow Mr. Steno has 5, and she has 12. / They split their money in half. She gets 2/3, and he gets 1/3. Do you think that's fair? /

Jen and Ken went to Burger World to buy a big bag of burnt burgers. On the way home, the bag / broke; and they spilled their burgers all over the highway. A policeman came by and asked them if they had / any cola (KO/HRA) and fries.

Please refer to section (B) of the complaint (KPLAEUPBT) and read all the way through to section (E). You'll note that / sections (R), (Q), and (T) are in error. They will have to be corrected before you type the final draft. / Please hurry.

What authority do you have to tell me what to do? You have no authority at all. / I'm going to call the policeman who lives in the apartment above me and ask him to come down and / talk to you.

Please indicate on your application your age, your sex, your weight (WAEUGT), your height (HAOEUGT), the color of / your hair and eyes, and your size. We will have your gown ready for you by the time you graduate / (TKPWRAD/WAET). Do you want a black gown with a white stripe or a white gown with a black stripe? Most of / the people I know are getting a red neon (TPHE/KWROPB) gown with an orange stripe.

Please bring your certificate when you come / up on stage to get your diploma (TKEU/PHROE/PHA). We'll give you your certificate when you reach 225 words a minute. / Maybe you can reach it by tomorrow. You'll plan to take the speed take on Monday or Tuesday, won't / you? If not, let me know if you want to take it on Thursday or Friday. You can't take / it on Wednesday because I'll be out of town. We do not have classes on Saturday or Sunday. Let me / know as soon as possible.

UNIT 10
DRILL XIX (Lessons 37-38)

Word Drill

☞ Review the following until you can write them without hesitation:

bath PWATD	cloth KRHOTD	breathe PWRAOETD
truth TRAOUTD	smother SPHOTD/KWRER	faith TPAEUTD
youth KWRAOUTD	breath PWRETD	death TKETD
filth TPEUL/AETD	clothe KHROETD	moth PHOTD
mouth PHOUTD	teeth TAOETD	tooth TAOTD
sooth SAOTD	leather HRETD/KWRER	cost KOSZ
lost HROSZ	last HRAESZ	fast TPAESZ
frost TPROSZ	quest KWESZ	trust TRUSZ
exist SKPEUSZ	midst PHEUD/AESZ	dusk TKUSZ
blast PWHRAESZ	mist PHEUSZ	task TASZ
risk REUSZ	flask TPHRASZ	whisk WHEUSZ
desk TKESZ	mask PHASZ	chasm KHASZ
spasm SPASZ	prism PREUSZ	sarcasm SAR/KASZ
dualism TKAOUL/SKPWEUPL	dualist TKAOUL/KWREUSZ	truism TRAOU/SKPWEUPL
truest TRAOUSZ		

Short Form Drill

☞ Review the following until you can write them without hesitation:

other OTD	another TPHOTD	either ETD	mother PHOETD
father TPATD	brother PWROTD	further TPRUTD	farther TPRATD
bother PWOTD	neither TPHAOETD	gather TKPWATD	rather RATD
together TOTD	although HR-TD	health HETD	method PH-TD
wealth WETD	earth R-TD	birth PWR-TD	forth TPR-TD
whether WH-TD	weather W-TD	width WEUTD	length HRAETD
depth TKP-TD	breadth PWRAETD	anybody TPHEUB	anyone TPHEUPB
anything TPHEUPBG	everybody KWR-B	everyone KWR-PB	everything KWR-PBG
anyhow TPHEUFD	anymore TPHEUPL	anyway TPHEUFPL	anyplace TPHEUPS
anywhere TPEUFRP	everyplace KWR-PS	everywhere KWR-FRP	everyday KWR-D
satisfy S-F	satisfaction S-FBGS	satisfactory S-FR	satisfying S-FG
secretary SEBG	season SAEPB	suppose SPOEZ	signature STPHAOUR
sister STER	disk STKEUBG	disc TKEUSZ	dust TKUS
first TPEURT			

Miscellaneous Drill

☞ Review the following until you can write them without hesitation:

I	RO–RBGS/1	VII	RO–RBGS/7	XV	RO–RBGS/15
II	RO–RBGS/2	VIII	RO–RBGS/8	XX	RO–RBGS/20
III	RO–RBGS/3	IX	RO–RBGS/9	XXIV	RO–RBGS/24
IV	RO–RBGS/4	X	RO–RBGS/10	XXX	RO–R BGS/30
V	RO–RBGS/5	XI	RO–RBGS/11	L	RO–RBGS/50
VI	RO–RBGS/6	XII	RO–RBGS/12	LX	RO–RBGS/0EU6

Practical Exercise

☞ Practice the following:

Have you ever had a muscle spasm? It is very, very painful (PAEUPB/FAUL). If you go to a doctor, he might send / you to the hospital. If he sends you to the hospital, they may have to take some x-rays. If they / do some x-rays, they may want you to exercise the spasm.

Are you willing to risk your entire fortune / on a game of chance? I hope not. It wouldn't be worth (WR–TD) it. My father used to tell me not to / gamble (TKPWAPL/PWAEL) away my life--what a truism! Everyone should listen to my dad's advice.

Anybody can do it if they try. Anyone / can try it if they do. I'll trust you if you trust in me. The deer run fast at dusk. / I'm not satisfied with my grade. I think I'll try harder.

This is my family sketch: my father is / 42; his name is Norman (TPHOR/PHAEPB). He works as a carpenter (KAR/PEPB/TER). My mother just turned 40. Her name is Jill. / She works in a bakery. My brother Ed goes to school. He is a senior. My sister Sue is a / lifeguard at the local pool. My cat, Steno, is a nuisance (TPHAOUS/KWRAPBS). She loves to scratch the chair. I also have / a brother Fred who is away in the service. He is on a boat in the ocean (OEGS). I used to have / a dog, Rover, but he ran away when my sister Sue took fiddle (TPEUD/AEL) lessons. We haven't seen him since.

Will / you please see my secretary today and ask her where the certificate is that you are supposed to sign? If / she can't find the document, have her go to the main office and see if she can locate a copy / of the paper. If not, we'll have to start all over again.

I keep all of my stuff in my desk. / My desk is where I keep all of the things that I consider necessary. I keep all of my credit / cards, my money, my toothpaste and my hairbrush in my desk.

Please put the disk on the desk / at dusk. Watch the weather forecast on TV and tell me whether it's going to snow or rain tomorrow. / I need to know so that I know what to wear outside. If it rains, I'll wear my raincoat; if it / snows, I'll wear my new winter coat. If it's going to be sunny, I'll wear my new bathing suit to / the beach.

Anybody who wants to go swimming with me can go any time. All they have to do is / tell me when they want to go. I'm leaving at 1:24 to pick up Peg and her brother Todd. / Want to go with us? We're going to have a picnic. The pool is in the park. Bring a friend / if you want to.

You'd better be careful in this weather, or you'll catch the flu. If you catch the / flu, you'll have a cold and sneeze all over the place. Then you'll have a fever and you won't be / able to go to school. Take care.

Don't bother me when I'm with my brother. My father and mother / let me go farther than I'd ever been before on an airplane alone. They let me go to France last / summer. I stayed with my cousin, Suzette (SAOU/SKPWAET). Their family took me all over France to see the many sights. It / was fabulous (TPAB/HROUS). I can't wait to go again. Maybe next summer.

I bought a new leather chair for the living / room. It is tan and has a green stripe on one side and a red stripe on the other. My mother / and father don't like it. My brother hates it. My cat, Heidi (HAOEUD/KWRAOE), loves it. She sleeps in it all day long. / She scratched it the other day and we found that it was stuffed with feathers.

Here are a few / things that I have been thinking about lately: Why is a moth drawn to a flame? Why is the sky / up? Why are teeth white? When there's a frost, why can you see breath? When the sun is shining, why can't / you see breath? Can we breathe in and out at the same time? Why do we yawn?

Do you have any / faith in your brother? How about your sister? Trust your family. The truth is, your family will help you. Never / underestimate the power of your family.

Word Drill

☞ Review the following until you can write them without hesitation:

jump SKWRUPL/AEP	pump PUPL/AEP	champ KHAPL/AEP
skimp SKEUPL/AEP	stamp STAPL/AEP	swamp SWAPL/AEP
milk PHEUL/AEBG	silk SEUL/AEBG	folk TPOEL/AEBG
talk TAUBG	walk WAUBG	chalk KHAUBG
film TPEUL/AEPL	realm REL/AEPL	helm HEL/AEPL
calm KAUPL	palm PAUPL	psalm SAUPL
lunch HRUPB/AEFP	bunch PWUPB/AEFP	branch PWRAPB/AEFP
bench PWEPB/AEFP	crunch KRUPB/AEFP	ranch RAPB/AEFP
foremost TPOER/PHOESZ	enterprise EPBT/PRAOEUZ	downtime TKOFRP/TAOEUPL
superdome SAOUP/TKOEPL	overdone OEFR/TKOEPB	postman POESZ./PHAEPB
undercut UPBD/KUT	booklet PWAOBG/HRAET	stairway STAEUR/WAEFPL
happier HAP/KWRAER	happiest HAP/KWRAESZ	crazier KRAEUZ/KWRAER
craziest KRAEUZ/KWRAESZ	busier PWEUZ/KWRAER	busiest PWEUZ/KWRAESZ
superior SAOUP/KWRAOR	savior SAEUFB/KWRAOR	closure KHROEZ/KWRUR
posture POS/TAOUR	denture TKEPBT/KWRUR	leisure HRAOEZ/KWRUR
jealous SKWREL/KWROUS	ambitious APL/PWEURBS	baptize PWAP/TAOEUZ
characterize KAEURBGT/KWRAOEUZ	materialize TAOERL/KWRAOEUZ	indicative EUPB/TKEUBG/TEUFB
sensitize SEPBS/TAOEUZ	sensitive SEPBS/TEUFB	beta PWET/KWRA (1)
coca KOEBG/KWRA	cola KOEL/KWRA	coma KOEPL/KWRA
comma KOPL/KWRA	soda SOED/KWRA	mama PHA/PHA
visa SRAOEZ/KWRA	semi SEPH/KWRAOEU	anti APBT/KWRAOEU
taxi TAFRPB/KWRAOE	khaki KABG/KWRAOE	mini PHEUPB/KWRAOE
maxi PHAFRPB/KWRAOE	echo EBG/KWROE	hero HER/KWROE
limo HREUPL/KWROE	taco TABG/KWROE	typo TAOEUP/KWROE
steno STEPB/KWROE	cafe KAF/KWRAEU	acne ABG/TPHAOE
acme ABG/PHAOE	coffee KOF/KWRAOE	movie PHOFB/KWRAOE

(1) Some words may be written differently, according to their syllabic division. For example, "beta" could be written PWE/TA, "cola" could be written KO/HRA, and so on.

Short Form Drill

☞ Review the following until you can write them without hesitation:

nobody TPHOEB	no one TPH-PB	nothing TPHOPBG	somebody SPH-B
someone SPH-PB	something SPH-PBG	nohow TPHOEFD	no way TPHOEFPL
nowhere TPHOEFRP	somehow SPH-FD	some way SPH-FPL	somewhere SPH-FRP
someday SPH-D	someplace SPH-PS	somewhat SWA	sometime SPH-T
sometimes SPH-TS	search SEFP	church KH-FP	answer SWER
individual SREUD	maximum PH-FRPB	correspondence KROPBS	Mr. PHR-
Mrs. PHR-S	Ms. PH-Z	Miss PH-S	person PERPB
personal PERPBL			

Miscellaneous Drill

☞ Review the following until you can write them without hesitation:

January SKWRA-FPLT	February TPE-FPLT	March PHA-FPLT
April A-FPLT	May PHAEU-FPLT	June SKWRAOU-FPLT
July SKWRU-FPLT	August AU-FPLT	September SE-FPLT
October O-FPLT	November TPHO-FPLT	December TKE-FPLT

Practical Exercise

☞ Practice the following:

The rock group will be in our city on January 24, 1995. They will then fly to Denver for a / performance on February 11; then on March 4, they will be in Memphis (PHEPL/FEUS) for the entire month. They will be / on tour in Europe (AOURP) during the Months of April, May, and June. They will then come back to America / for a big celebration on July 4 and then take the rest of July, all of August, and part of / September off to be with their family. In October they will be in South (SOUTD) America; in November, they will be / in Germany (SKWERPL/TPHAEFPL); and then in December, home again.

What does the future hold for you? Can you see into / the future? I can't. If I could, I would hope you could see nothing but goodness and happiness--no / sadness!

Where would this world be without the comma? The comma is very, very necessary in writing what we say. / Without the comma, we might all be very, very confused (KOPB/FAOUZ/AED).

There's a right way and a wrong way to order / from a menu (PHE/TPHAOU). If you had a choice between tacos, hamburgers, hot dogs, steak, and surf and turf, which would / you take? I'd take the salad (SAL/AED) because I love green, leafy things. Would you rather have coffee, tea, milk, soda, / or water?

Which one in your family is the happiest? Which one is the craziest? Which one is the busiest? / You, your mother, or your father? Is your cat or your dog happier? Is your bird or your fish crazier? Is / your brother or your sister busier?

Now, you can buy a book on how to do anything. I bought a / little booklet the other day that told me how to go fast on the steno machine. The title (TAOEULT) was "How to / get to 225 in 10 easy steps." I learned a lot from it, but I'm still at 60. I / know it takes time, so I'll keep trying until I get to 225. I'll keep practicing every day. /

Keep these thoughts foremost in your mind: never give up, keep your nose to the grindstone (TKPWRAOEUPBD/STOEPB), practice every day, and / enjoy what you do. Enjoy your practice time.

I used to pump gas for a living. I can remember one / day when I pumped over 500 gallons of gas in an hour. It was on July 16, 1990, / from 10:06 a.m. until 11:06 a.m. I remember because we were having a sale on gas that / day. It was only 25 cents a gallon. What a bargain. I never pumped so much gas in my life. /

Please choose one of the following days and times when you would like to have your picture (TAOUR) taken. March 15 / at 9:35 a.m., April 4 at 11:06 a.m., July 30 at 2:24 p.m., or November 12 at 12 noon. / Please choose one now and let me know.

What did you do with the correspondence I gave to my secretary? / I need to put a stamp on one of the envelopes, and I can't find it. It is a big, / white envelope, about 11 inches by 22 inches. I think I'll have to put an extra stamp or two on / the envelope because it is so large. What do you think?

The speed limit (HREUPLT) in this town is only 30 / miles an hour. The speed limit on the highway is 55 miles an hour. The speed limit in class / is 225 words per minute. Please don't exceed (SKPAOED) the speed limit.

You need to check off your title (TAOEULT): Mr., Mrs., / Miss, or Ms. You also need to check off your sex: male or female; and fill in your date of birth. / We need one more thing: What is your name?

Have you ever starched something that was silk? I did. What / a mess. I got too much starch in the silk; and, now, it is stiff. I can't even bend it. / I tried to take some of the starch out by soaking it in hot water, but after it dried (TKRAOEUD), it / became rigid again. Can you help me?

A cat watched a bird on a perch in a birch tree. The bird / watched the cat who sat on the ground. They stared at each other for 16 hours until the cat jumped up / and the bird flew away.

Nobody doesn't like Sara (SA/RA) Lee. Everybody loves her. She makes the best cookies (KAOBG/KWRAOEZ) in town. / My favorite is chocolate (KHOBG/HRAET) chip.

The following people are wanted by the police: Mr. and Mrs. John Smith, Mr. Ed Jones, / Miss Karen (KAEURPB) Pierce, and Ms. "M." Mr. and Mrs. Smith are wanted for robbery; Mr. Jones is wanted for speeding; / Miss Pierce stole something; and Ms. "M" escaped from jail.

Word Drill

☞ Practice the following until you can write them without hesitation. Notice that the outlines are given in their English equivalent for letters that required combinations (A/DRES, not A/TKRES):

address A/DRES	Patrick PAT/RIK	Spring KI-RBGS/SPRING
Washington WASH/~~AEG~~/TON	Denton DEN/TON	George JORJ
Slatery SLAT/RAEY	peanut PE/NUT	butter BUT/YER
employed PLOID	explain SKPLAIN	secret SE/KRET
calorie KAL/RAOE	artificial ART/FISHL	candy KAND/AEY
tastes TAISZ/AEZ	understanding SDAND/AEG	infringed IN/FRIFJ/AED
Reese's RAOES/AOS	Pieces KI-RBGS/PAOES/AEZ	accused A/KAOUS/AED
formula FORM/LA	inside NAOID	outside OUD
quite KWAOIT	future FAOUR	ingredient IN/GRAOED/YENT
contained ~~KON~~/TAIND	flavoring FLAIFRG	discovered SDOFRD
growing GROW/AEG	berry BER/AEY	diameter DAOIM/TER
harvest HAR/VESZ	distinct SDIFKT	blue BLAOU
initials NISHLZ	factory FAKT/RAEY	

Short Form Drill

☞ Review the following until you can write them without hesitation:

total TOELT	tonight TONT	testimony TEM
specific SPEFK	standard STARD	zero ZROE
respect R-S	result RULT	ready R-D
really R-L	reason RAOEN	reasonably RAOEBL
recognize ROZ	regular REG	recommend ROM
require RAOIR	agency AGS	agent AGT
careful KAIF	carried K-RD	federal FRAL
carefully KAIFL	guilty G-Y	issue ISH (EURB)
listen LIFN	future FAOUR	picture TAOUR
local LOEL	purpose PURP	question KWE
positive POZ	possibly POBL	U. S. UZ
United States NAITS		

Miscellaneous Drill

☞ Review the following until you can write them without hesitation:

one WUPB	two TWO	three THRAOE	four TPOUR
five TPAOIV	six SIX	seven SEV	eight AIGT
nine NAOIN	ten TEN	eleven LEV	twelve TWEFL
thirteen THAOEN	fourteen FRAOEN	fifteen FAOEN	sixteen XAOEN
seventeen VAOEN	eighteen AOEN	nineteen NAOEN	twenty TWEY
thirty THIY	forty FROY	fifty FIY	sixty SIY
seventy SEY	eighty AIY	ninety NAOIY	

twenty-one TWEY/WUN	forty-one FROY/WUN
twenty-two TWEY/TWO	forty-two FROY/TWO
twenty-three TWEY/THRAOE	forty-three FROY/THRAOE
twenty-four TWEY/FOUR	forty-four FROY/FOUR
twenty-five TWEY/FAOIV	forty-five FROY/FAOIV
twenty-six TWEY/SIX	forty-six FROY/SIX
twenty-seven TWEY/SEV	forty-seven FROY/SEV
twenty-eight TWEY/AIGT	forty-eight FROY/AIGT
twenty-nine TWEY/NAOIN	forty-nine FROY/NAOIN
thirty-one THIY/WUN	fifty-one FIY/WUN
thirty-two THIY/TWO	fifty-two FIY/TWO
thirty-three THIY/THRAOE	fifty-three FIY/THRAOE
thirty-four THIY/FOUR	fifty-four FIY/FOUR
thirty-five THIY/FAOIV	fifty-five FIY/FAOIV
thirty-six THIY/SIX	fifty-six FIY/SIX
thirty-seven THIY/SEV	fifty-seven FIY/SEV
thirty-eight THIY/AIGT	fifty-eight FIY/AIGT
thirty-nine THIY/NAOIN	fifty-nine FIY/NAOIN

Dear Sir D-S	Dear Mr. DMR-
Dear Mrs. DMR-S	Dear Ms. DM-Z
Dear Miss DM-S	Dear Madam D-M
Ladies and Gentlemen LAJ	Gentlemen JE-FPLT
Gentlemen and Ladies JAL	To whom it may concern TWERN

Practical Exercise

☞ Practice the following:

Q   Please state your full name and address for the record, sir.

A   My name is Patrick J. Spring, and I live / at 222 Washington Street here in Denton.

Q   And how old are you, please, sir?

A   I am 42 years old. /

Q   And can you tell us why you are here today before this Court and jury?

A   Yes, sir. I am here to / give testimony. I have been called as a witness on behalf of the defendant in this case, Mr. George Slatery. /

Q   And what is it that Mr. Slatery does for a living?

A   Mr. Slatery is the president of the Tasty Peanut / Butter Company in Denton.

Q   Are you employed by the Tasty Company?

A   Yes, sir, I am. I am their chief / researcher.

Q   What do you do as their head researcher? Please explain what your regular job might entail?

A   Well, it's my job / to make sure that everything follows a good standard. I also do top secret research and experiments with respect to new / products. I was responsible for coming up with the no-calorie peanut butter cup as well as many other products. / I also developed a new artificial peanut candy that looks, smells and tastes like the real thing.

Q   I see. And / can you tell us why you are here today, Mr. Spring?

A   Yes. It is my understanding that Mr. Slatery has / been served a notice that he has infringed on the patent for making a candy called Reese's Pieces. He has been / accused of copying their formula for making those tiny little candies that have peanut butter on the inside and a / hard shell on the outside. A U. S. agent arrested him last week.

Q   I see. And can you tell me how / you are involved in this case. What is the reason that you were called to give testimony tonight? And please / be specific, sir.

A   Yes, sir. As the head researcher and developer, it was my job to create a type of / candy that was similar in taste and texture to this other candy, possibly creating a whole new / type of candy.

Q   And did you indeed do that, sir? Did you make a candy that was quite similar to the / Reese's Pieces candy?

A   Yes, sir. I did. I was very successful in coming up with our own candy called / Tasty Pieces. The whole purpose of my job was to recommend new types of candies that we possibly could use / in the future, using regular things to make the candy.

Q   Please listen to the question very carefully. Did you use / any of the secret ingredients that are contained in this other candy?

A   No, sir. I did not. In fact, I / can tell you exactly what goes into my Tasty Pieces if you like.

Q   Yes, please tell us what it is / that you use to make your Tasty Pieces.

A   Well, sir, to begin with, we use a completely artificial / peanut flavoring that is made up of a newly discovered plant that we created. This plant is called a peanut / plant and we have been successful in growing a new type of berry called the peanut berry. This berry / is very small to begin with; but when it is ripe, it is the exact size and diameter of the / Reese's Pieces.

Q   Are you ready to tell us what you did with this peanut berry, sir?

A   We carefully harvest the / berries until they are ripe, and then we pick the berries, clean them, and then cover them with a hard / candy shell.

Q   Do they really require careful harvesting?

A   Yes, sir. They do.

Q   What is the total amount of peanut berries / you can harvest in one day?

A   About 245,694, if we don't have a frost.

Q   And if you have a / frost, how many can you pick in a day?

A   Zero.

Q   Do you use local people to pick your berries?

A   Yes, / sir.

Q   Are these people who live in the United States?

A   Yes, sir.

Q   Are you positive about that, sir?

A   Yes, sir. We / might possibly use other people, but most of them are born in the United States.

Q   Have you ever been contacted / by a member of a federal agency concerning the fact that you carried no insurance covering your workers?

A   No, sir, / I have not.

Q   Has a federal agent ever talked to you about pleading guilty to fraud concerning these peanut berries? /

A   Yes, sir. There was an agent who called my office one day and said he would like to talk about / berry fraud. He said the issue was one of fraud and deceit. I told him that I was not going / to plead guilty and that he should contact my lawyer.

Q   I see. Now, let me go to a different picture / now. Can you tell me the color that you used to cover your peanut berries with, sir, and what color / is used in the Reese's Pieces.

A   Yes. I believe the Reese's Pieces are a yellow and orange color while / our Tasty Pieces are a very distinct black and blue. In addition, we have a very fine "TP" printed on / each Tasty Piece.

Q   And does the "TP" in fact stand for "Tasty Pieces."

A   No, sir. It does not; however, that's / not a bad idea.

Q   Well, what does the "TP" stand for then, sir?

A   Those are the initials for Tom Pierce, the / man who makes the candy in our factory.

UNIT 11
DRILL XXII (Lessons 43-44)

Word Drill

☞ Practice the following until you can write them without hesitation:

occupation KAOUPGS	Donald DON/YALD	McDonald MAK/DON/YALD
burger BURG/YER	title TAOILT	around ARND
yearly YAOERL	subscription SUB/SKRIPGS	largest LARJ/YESZ
bigger BIG/YER	absolutely SLAOUL	producing PROUS/AEG
decided SDAOID/AED	sue SAOU	parties PART/YAOEZ
suit SAOUT	threaten THRET/YEN	aware A/WAIR
clue KHRAOU	spelled SPELD	seal SAOEL
addition A/DIGS	installment IN/STAL/MAENT	balance BAL
communication K-MGS	litigation LIT/GAIGS	

Short Form Drill

☞ Review the following until you can write them without hesitation:

position ZIGS	physical F-L	okay OK
official FISHL	record RORD	refund REFN
purchase PR-CH	proper PROR	national NAL
negligence NEGS	negligent NEGT	contain TAIN
happen HAP	happening HAPG	interest TR-
anger GER	contact KAKT	contract KRAKT
invest VEFT	invoice VOI	involve VOFL
magazine MAZ	matter M-T	members MEBZ
remove R-V	remain R-M	president PREZ
	receipt RAOET	receive RAOEV
organization ORGS	situate SWAIT	situation SWAIGS

66

Miscellaneous Drill

☞ Review the following until you can write them without hesitation:

sixty-one SIY/WUN	eighty-one AIY/WUN
sixty-two SIY/TWO	eighty-two AIY/TWO
sixty-three SIY/THRAOE	eighty-three AIY/THRAOE
sixty-four SIY/FOUR	eighty-four AIY/FOUR
sixty-five SIY/FAOIV	eighty-five AIY/FAOIV
sixty-six SIY/SIX	eighty-six AIY/SIX
sixty-seven SIY/SEV	eighty-seven AIY/SEV
sixty-eight SIY/AIGT	eighty-eight AIY/AIGT
sixty-nine SIY/NAOIN	eighty-nine AIY/NAOIN
seventy-one SEY/WUN	ninety-one NAOIY/WUN
seventy-two SEY/TWO	ninety-two NAOIY/TWO
seventy-three SEY/THRAOE	ninety-three NAOIY/THRAOE
seventy-four SEY/FOUR	ninety-four NAOIY/FOUR
seventy-five SEY/FAOIV	ninety-five NAOIY/FAOIV
seventy-six SEY/SIX	ninety-six NAOIY/SIX
seventy-seven SEY/SEV	ninety-seven NAOIY/SEV
seventy-eight SEY/AIGT	ninety-eight NAOIY/AIGT
seventy-nine SEY/NAOIN	ninety-nine NAOIY/NAOIN
hundred HUND	thousand THOUS
million MLON	billion BLON
trillion TRON	zillion ZON

sincerely S-Y	sincerely yours S-YZ	yours sincerely Y-S
respectfully R-Y	respectfully yours R-YZ	yours respectfully Y-R
cordially K-Y	cordially yours K-YZ	yours cordially Y-K
truly T-Y	truly yours T-YZ	yours truly Y-T
very sincerely V-S	very respectfully V-R	very cordially V-K
very truly V-RT	very truly yours VE/T-YZ	

Practical Exercise

☞ Practice the following:

Q Would you please tell us your name and occupation?
A Yes. My name is Donald McDonald, and I am connected / with Burger World, Incorporated.
Q What is your position with Burger World?
A I am currently the president.
Q What is your official / title, sir?
A Chief chef.

Q   Okay. And as chief chef of Burger World, did you happen to be involved in the / making of a contract with a national organization called Better Burgers?

A   Yes, sir. I did.

Q   And how did you happen to get / involved with this situation?

A   Well, early last year, around the 15th of April, I happened to get a phone call / from the organization president asking me if I would invest $50,000 in the company. I told him I might have / an interest, but that I would want to know what I would receive for my money.

Q   And what did he / tell you, sir?

A   He said that I would be in receipt of a yearly subscription to their magazine and I / would also be entitled to free legal advice from their corporation. He also said that I would be a member of / one of the largest organizations that dealt with making the world a better place by producing bigger and better burgers / for the buck.

Q   I see. Okay. And can you tell me what you actually received after you became a member / of Better Burgers?

A   Nothing, nothing. I received absolutely nothing.

Q   Did you, in fact, pay $50,000 for a share in the / company called Better Burgers.

A   Yes, sir. I did. For the record, I was asked to purchase 50 shares at $1,000 / a share. I became a member by paying $25,000 cash and another $25,000 six months later.

Q   Now, concerning the matter / of your membership in the Better Burger Society, did you let the president know of your anger after you said / you received nothing?

A   Yes, sir, I did. I contacted the organization and asked that my name be removed / from their list of members. I then told the president that I would call my lawyer and ask for a / refund for all the money I paid into the organization.

Q   Okay. Then what happened?

A   That is when I decided that / I sue them for negligence. I think they were very, very negligent in the whole thing.

Q   Did you have any physical / contact with any of the parties in this suit? Did you threaten any of the defendants in this case? /

A   No, sir, I did not. I tried not to put myself in a position where I would lose my anger. / I more or less stayed away from them and tried to remain calm. I let my lawyer do all the / talking.

Q   Okay. When did you first become aware that things were not proper? When did it become known to you that something / wrong was happening or about to happen?

A   I think my first clue was the invoice that I received from Better / Burger stating that they were in receipt of my money.

Q   Tell us what was wrong with that invoice, sir.

A   Well, / to begin with, they spelled my name wrong. They also did not have the proper dates on the invoice. The / amount of money I gave them was wrong on the invoice. And the official seal of the company was missing. / In addition, they spelled the word "burger" incorrectly.

Q   How much did the receipt say you paid?

A $4,000.

Q   And how / much did you, in fact, pay?

A   My first installment was $25,000.

Q   I see. Go ahead. Tell us what happened / next.

A   And when I asked them to correct the amount, they told me I had to pay the balance. I / told them they better remove my name from their list of members and that I was going to tear up / the contract I had with them.

Q   Was this the most recent communication you have had with Better Burger?
A   Yes, sir. / I believe so. I basically told them that I did not want to remain a member of Better Burger because / I didn't agree with their organization.
Q   And what did you do about the matter?
A   I decided to contact my lawyer / and let him handle everything.
Q   And that is when you contacted me; right?
A   Yes, sir.
Q   Can you tell me this, / Mr. McDonald, how many burgers do you make a year at Burger World?
A   Well, I would estimate that we probably make close / to 50 million burgers a year.
Q   That's a lot of burgers.
A   Yes, sir. It is.
Q   Why did you feel the / need to join an organization like Better Burger?
A   I thought it would be a good investment; I guess I was / wrong.
Q   Did you ever get proper satisfaction?
A   No, sir.
Q   Did you ever get a refund of the money you spent? /
A   No, sir.
Q   How much are you seeking in this litigation?
A $98 million.

Word Drill

☞ Practice the following until you can write them without hesitation:

aware A/WAIR	hearing HAERG	commission KMIGS
action ABGS	matter M-T	conducted KUKT/AED
beginning GING	danger DAIFJ/YER	jeopardized JEP/DAOIZ/AED
teachers TAOECH/YERZ	experiment SKPAOERMT	entail EN/TAIL
board BORD	homework HOEM/AE/WORK (1)	project PROJ
assigned A/SAOIN/AED	continue T-N	successful SES/FAUL
forced FORS/AED	courses KOURS/AEZ	information N-FRMGS
immediate MAOED	data DAT	exchange SKPAIJ
university AOUFRT	Iceland AOISZ/LAEND (2)	graduate GRAUT

(1) A distinction can be made by writing WAORK for "work" or by placing the AE between the words to join them together.

(2) A distinction can be made by writing LAEND for "land" or by placing the AE between the words to join them together.

Short Form Drill

☞ Review the following until you can write them without hesitation:

subject SUJ	success SES	superintendent SAOUPT	research R-CH
testify TEF	respond SPOND	observe ZEFRB	operate PRAIT
representation REPGS	qualify KWAUF	regard RARD	occasion KAIGS
perhaps PRAPS	city STI	children KHIRN	control KROEL
contribute KRIBT	comfort K-FRT	communicate K-MT	general J-N
classify KL-F	communication K-MGS	character KAIRK	under DER
convenience VAOENS	convenient VAOENT	understand SDAND	understood SDAOD

Miscellaneous Drill

☞ Review the following until you can write them without hesitation:

1st 1/AESZ	26th 26/AETD	51st 15EU/AESZ	76th EU67/AETD
2nd 2/AEND	27th 27/AETD	52nd 25EU/AEND	77th EU7/AETD
3rd 3/AERD	28th 28/AETD	53rd 35EU/AERD	78th 78/AETD
4th 4/AETD	29th 29/AETD	54th 45EU/AETD	79th 79/AETD
5th 5/AETD	30th 30/AETD	55th 5EU/AETD	80th 0EU8/AETD
6th 6/AETD	31st 13EU/AESZ	56th 56/AETD	81st 1EU8/AESZ
7th 7/AETD	32nd 23EU/AESZ	57th 57/AETD	82nd 2EU8/AEND
8th 8/AETD	33rd 3EU/AERD	58th 58/AETD	83rd 3EU8/AERD
9th 9/AETD	34th 34/AETD	59th 59/AETD	84th 4EU8/AETD
10th 10/AETD	35th 35/AETD	60th 0EU6/AETD	85th 5EU8/AETD
11th 1EU/AETD	36th 36/AETD	61st 1EU6/AESZ	86th 6EU8/AETD
12th 12/AETD	37th 37/AETD	62nd 2EU6/AEND	87th EU78/AETD
13th 13/AETD	38th 38/AETD	63rd 3EU6/AERD	88th EU8/AETD
14th 14/AETD	39th 39/AETD	64th 4eu6/AETD	89th 89/AETD
15th 15/AETD	40th 40/AETD	65th 5EU6/AETD	90th 0EU9/AETD
16th 16/AETD	41st 14EU/AESZ	66th EU6/AETD	91st 1EU9/AESZ
17th 17/AETD	42nd 24EU/AEND	67th 67/AETD	92nd 2EU9/AEND
18th 18/AETD	43rd 34EU/AERD	68th 68/AETD	93rd 3EU9/AERD
19th 19/AETD	44th 4EU/AETD	69th 69/AETD	94th 4EU9/AETD
20th 20/AETD	45th 45/AETD	70th 0EU7/AETD	95th 5EU9/AETD
21st 12EU/AESZ	46th 46/AETD	71st 1EU7/AESZ	96th EU69/AETD
22nd 2EU/AEND	47th 47/AETD	72nd 2EU7/AEND	97th EU79/AETD
23rd 23/AERD	48th 48/AETD	73rd 3EU7/AERD	98th EU89/AETD
24th 24/AETD	49th 49/AETD	74th 4EU7/AETD	99th EU9/AETD
25th 25/AETD	50th 50/AETD	75th 5EU7/AETD	100th 1/HND/AETD

North NORT	northeast NAOESZ	northwest NOESZ	South SOUTD
southeast SAOESZ	southwest SWESZ	East AOESZ	West WESZ

Practical Exercise

☞ Practice the following:

Q   Now, as you are aware, the subject matter of this hearing before this commission is in regard to an action by / the superintendent of schools for the city school district. Mr. Fenton, you are the superintendent of schools; and as such, / you are here in regard to this matter?

A   Yes, sir. I am.

Q   And will you please tell us why you / are here today to testify?

A   Yes, sir. I am here because I have been asked to respond to a research / project that was conducted by six of the teachers for our school district.

Q   Can you be a little bit more / specific, sir? What exactly did this research project entail?

A   Well, it was understood from the beginning that at no time would / the children be in any danger, the comfort and safety of the children would never be jeopardized. We had someone / observe the children at all times.

Q   Please answer the question, Mr. Fenton, what did this experiment involve?

A   Well, if I / may qualify my answer by saying that we had the complete control of the situation, we did not know that anything / was going to go wrong.

Q   Mr. Fenton, please respond to my question, what did this research project entail?

A   Well, perhaps / I should start at the beginning.

Q   Yes, please do so, if that is convenient.

A   It all started about two years / ago when a group of students came to the school board meeting wanting to know if they could have control / of how much homework they would be assigned each night.

Q   Please continue.

A   Well, we told them that it was out / of the question. However, last year, a number of teachers presented a program that allowed the students to pick and / choose the homework they did each night. The teachers said that they would conduct an experiment with a control group / and see if the project was a success.

Q   And can you tell us any of the results of the / research project? Do you know what the results were?

A   Yes, sir. In general, the students who were allowed to pick what / homework they had appeared to be much more successful than the other students.

Q   I see. Did you observe any other / results?

A   Yes. The children who were forced to do the homework that the teachers assigned, in general, failed the courses. /

Q   Why was that, sir?

A   I really don't know. I began to classify the students who conducted their own homework assignments / as better students, but I found that not true in all cases.

Q   Do I understand you to say that all / of the children who decided what their own homework was performed better than those children who were forced to do / homework assigned by the teacher?

A   Yes, sir.

Q   I see. Did you communicate this information to any of the other board / members? Did you have occasion to share your findings with anyone?

A   My only communication so far was an interview I granted / to one of the parents who works for the local paper. She wrote a story about the success of the program / and asked that we begin using this method in all courses.

Q   What was your response to that, Dr. Fenton?

A   We / basically said no, not until we do further research on the matter.

Q   I see. And that is why you are / here today; to tell us about the research project in greater detail?

A   Yes, sir. That is what I understand I / am to testify about. I am here to contribute as much information as I can about the facts.

Q   Tell me / this, Dr. Fenton, under whose control did the teachers operate?

A   They were under no one's immediate control.

Q   Did they answer / to anybody?

72

A   No.

Q   Was there a special group formed to put the data together?

A   No, sir.

Q   Who was the person / in charge of this whole project?

A   Well, I suppose if there was one person who was responsible for gathering most / of the data, it would be Ms. Osgood, our third grade teacher.

Q   Is she employed by the city school district? /

A   No, sir. She was here on an exchange program.

Q   And where is Ms. Osgood from, sir?

A   She came to us from / the University of Iceland, sir.

Q   And what is the success rate of children who graduate in the Iceland School District; / do you know, sir?

A   Yes, I do. They have a success rate of 100 percent.

Word Drill

☞ Practice the following until you can write them without hesitation:

begin GIN	action ABGS	involvement VOFL/MAENT
financial F-NL	agreeable GRAOEBL	dandy DAND/AEY
occupation KAOUPGS	Gerald JAIRLD	division DWIGS
CEO KR-FK/EFK/OFK	computer KPAOUT/YER	memorial ME/MORL
highway HOI	offering OFRG	build BILD
building BILD/AEG	Anderson AN/DER/SON	charge KHARJ
inquire KWIR	agreement GRAOEMT	options OPGS/AEZ
	lemon LEM/YON	decided SDAOID/AED
Anchorage AFK/RAJ	headquarters HED/KWART/YERZ	plastic PLAS/TIK
power POW/YER	doesn't DUNZ	cost KOSZ
retail RE/TAIL	business BIZ	

Short Form Drill

☞ Review the following until you can write them without hesitation:

emphasis EMS	emphasize EMZ	enable NAIBL	enclosure KLAOUR
enter NER	equal KWL-	general J-N	generally J-NL
indict DAOIT	industry STRI	inform N-FRM	initial NISHL
inquire KWIR	inquiry KWIR/AEY	insure NAOUR	outside OUD
inside NAOID	recommendation ROMGS	idea DA	area RA
acre AK	into NAO	unto UNT	onto ONT
very many VEM	too many TAOM	so many SOEM	how many HOUM
very much VECH	too much TAOCH	so much SOECH	how much HOUCH

Miscellaneous Drill

☞ Review the following until you can write them without hesitation:

first FIRT	tenth TETD	nineteenth NAOETD
second SEKD	eleventh LETD	twentieth TWEY/AETD
third THIRD	twelfth TWETD	thirtieth THIY/AETD
fourth FOTD	thirteenth THAOETD	fortieth FROY/AETD
fifth FITD	fourteenth FRAOETD	fiftieth FIY/AETD
sixth SITD	fifteenth FAOETD	sixtieth SIY/AETD
seventh SETD	sixteenth XAOETD	seventieth SEY/AETD
eighth AITD	seventeenth VAOETD	eightieth AIY/AETD
ninth NAOITD	eighteenth AOETD	ninetieth NAOIY/AETD

twenty-first TWEY/FIRT	forty-ninth FROY/NAOITD	seventy-eighth SEY/AITD
twenty-second TWEY/SEKD	fifty-first FIY/FIRT	seventy-ninth SEY/NAOITD
twenty-third TWEY/THIRD	fifty-second FIY/SEKD	eighty-first AIY/FIRT
twenty-fourth TWEY/FOTD	fifty-third FIY/THIRD	eighty-second AIY/SEKD
twenty-fifth TWEY/FITD	fifty-fourth FIY/FOTD	eighty-third AIY/THIRD
twenty-sixth TWEY/SITD	fifty-fifth FIY/FITH	eighty-fourth AIY/FOTD
twenty-seventh TWEY/SETD	fifty-sixth FIY/SITD	eighty-fifth AIY/FITD
twenty-eighth TWEY/AITD	fifty-seventh FIY/SETD	eighty-sixth AIY/SITD
twenty-ninth TWEY/NAOITD	fifty-eighth FIY/AITD	eighty-seventh AIY/SETD
thirty-first THIY/FIRT	fifty-ninth FIY/NAOITD	eighty-eighth AIY/AITD
thirty-second THIY/SEKD	sixty-first SIY/FIRT	eighty-ninth AIY/NAOITD
thirty-third THIY/THIRD	sixty-second SIY/SEKD	ninety-first NAOIY/FIRT
thirty-fourth THIY/FOTD	sixty-third SIY/THIRD	ninety-second NAOIY/SEKD
thirty-fifth THIY/FITD	sixty-fourth SIY/FOTD	ninety-third NAOIY/THIRD
thirty-sixth THIY SITD	sixty-fifth SIY/FITD	ninety-fourth NAOIY/FOTD
thirty-seventh THIY SETD	sixty-sixth SIY/SITD	ninety-fifth NAOIY/FITD
thirty-eighth THIY/AITD	sixty-seventh SIY/SETD	ninety-sixth NAOIY/SITD
thirty-ninth THIY/NAOITD	sixty-eighth SIY/AITD	ninety-seventh NAOIY/SETD
forty-first FROY/FIRT	sixty-ninth SIY/NAOITD	ninety-eighth NAOIY/AITD
forty-second FROY/SEKD	seventy-first SEY/FIRT	ninety-ninth NAOIY/NAOITD
forty-third FROY/THIRD	seventy-second SEY/SEKD	hundredth HUTD
forty-fourth FROY/FOTD	seventy-third SEY/THIRD	thousandth THOUTD
forty-fifth FROY/FITD	seventy-fourth SEY/FOTD	millionth MITD
forty-sixth FROY/SITD	seventy-fifth SEY/FITD	billionth BITD
fort-seventh FROY/SETD	seventy-sixth SEY/SITD	trillionth TRITD
forty-eighth FROY/AITD	seventy-seventh SEY/SETD	zillionth ZITD

Alabama A-FPLT/L-FPLT	Montana M-FPLT/T-FPLT
Alaska A-FPLT/K-FPLT	Nebraska N-FPLT/E-FPLT
Arizona A-FPLT/Z-FPLT	Nevada N-FPLT/V-FPLT
Arkansas A-FPLT/R-FPLT	New Hampshire N-FPLT/H-FPLT
California C-FPLT/A-FPLT	New Jersey N-FPLT/J-FPLT
Colorado C-FPLT/O-FPLT	New Mexico N-FPLT/M-FPLT
Connecticut KR-FPLT/T-FPLT	New York N-FPLT/Y-FPLT
Delaware D-FPLT/E-FPLT	North Carolina N-FPLT/C-FPLT
Florida F-FPLT/A-FPLT	North Dakota N-FPLT/D-FPLT
Georgia G-FPLT/A-FPLT	Ohio O-FPLT/H-FPLT
Hawaii H-FPLT/I-FPLT	Oklahoma O-FPLT/K-FPLT
Idaho I-FPLT/D-FPLT	Oregon O-FPLT/R-FPLT
Illinois I-FPLT/L-FPLT	Pennsylvania P-FPLT/A-FPLT
Indiana I-FPLT/N-FPLT	Rhode Island R-/FPLT/I-FPLT
Iowa I-FPLT/A-FPLT	South Carolina S-FPLT/C-FPLT
Kansas K-FPLT/S-FPLT	South Dakota S-FPLT/D-FPLT
Kentucky K-FPLT/Y-FPLT	Tennessee T-FPLT/N-FPLT
Louisiana L-FPLT/A-FPLT	Texas T-FPLT/X-FPLT
Maine M-FPLT/E-FPLT	Utah U-FPLT/T-TPLT
Maryland M-FPLT/D-FPLT	Vermont V-FPLT/T-FPLT
Massachusetts M-FPLT/A-FPLT	Virginia V-FPLT/A-FPLT
Michigan M-FPLT/I-FPLT	Washington W-FPLT/A-FPLT
Minnesota M-FPLT/N-FPLT	West Virginia W-FPLT/V-FPLT
Mississippi M-FPLT/S-FPLT	Wisconsin W-FPLT/I-FPLT
Missouri M-FPLT/O-FPLT	Wyoming W-FPLT/Y-FPLT

Practical Exercise

☞ Practice the following:

Q First, let us get the reason we are here on the record. To begin with, my name is Chester Gaul; / I am the lawyer for Mrs. Jamison, who is the plaintiff in this action. Generally, I am going to ask / you some questions regarding your involvement in a financial concern; is that agreeable with you, Mr. Quant?

A Yes, sir. / That's fine and dandy with me. I'll do my best to answer any question that you ask me. I'm very / much interested in getting this thing over with.

Q Very well. Now, would you please tell us your name / and address, and also your occupation?

A My name is Gerald A. Quant; I am the CEO for the / New York division of Quick Computer Company.

Q And your address, sir?

A My home address is 442 Memorial Highway, / Cincinnati, Ohio.

Q   Thank you, sir. Now, let me emphasize the fact that you are here under your own free will. / You have come here to tell us how much you know about offering of stock in the Quick Computer Company; / is that correct, sir?

A   Yes, sir.

Q   Tell me about the stock deal; will you, sir?

A   Okay. We had the idea / that we could raise enough money to build a new office building in Topeka, Kansas, if we could sell stock / in our company. John Anderson, our Vice President in charge of sales, began to inquire into the matter. He said / that we could enter into an agreement with another computer company and share our stock options.

Q   I see. What was / the name of this other industry?

A   It was Lemon Computers.

Q   And where were they based, sir?

A   Their main headquarters was / in Anchorage, Alaska.

Q   Can you tell us a little bit more about the initial agreement between Lemon and Quick?

A   Yes, / we decided to merge our offices and form one big company called Quick Lemon Computers. We wanted to put our / emphasis on making computers rather than selling them. We did not want to enter into the area of selling because / we didn't know how to price them. We figured we would ask too much or not very much. Generally, we / made computers and sold them to other companies.

Q   I see. I would like to inquire into your method of / making computers if I may. What goes into making a computer, generally speaking?

A   I'm sorry, sir, that information is top / secret.

Q   What type of enclosure do you use in making your computers?

A   We use a plastic case made of thin / plastic.

Q   What enables the computer to work?

A   I'm not sure, but I think it is a little chip inside.

Q   What / is the outside case made of again, sir?

A   Plastic.

Q   How do you insure that you don't have too much power / in your computer so it doesn't melt?

A   I don't know.

Q   How many hours go into the making of one computer? /

A   Generally speaking, about fifteen hours.

Q   Are there very many parts in the computers you make?

A   Not too many, no.

Q   How / much does one of your Lemon Quick Computers cost, sir?

A   The retail value is around $50.00

Q   Do you have / any idea what is inside your computers at all?

A   Not really. I leave that to the experts.

Q   How large of / a plant do you operate to make your computers, sir?

A   About an acre and a half.

Q   Are you an equal / partner with the other officers of your corporation?

A   Yes, sir. We all have equal shares.

Q   How many shares do you / have in Lemon Quick Computers, sir?

A   I have 16,000 shares.

Q   Did someone inform you of a lawsuit against / your company where an inquiry was being made into the fact that your computers don't work the way they should? /

A   Yes. Mr. Anderson called me at my office about three months ago and said that we were having problems with our / computers, so much so that we made a recommendation that we close down our plant and go out of business. /

Q   Did you take his advice, sir?

A   Not right away. I wanted to find out what the problems were before I / decided to close down. I ran into a friend who said he would enable us to fix our computers if we / did what he said.

Q   What did he recommend, sir?

A   That we use a steel shell on the outside of our / computers and that we put more chips inside and that we hang onto what we have already put into the / company.

PHRASE DRILL - A

☞ *learn the following:*

about a BAI	about the B-T	about you BAU	after the AFRT
are you RAU	before the B-FRT	can a KAI	can he KE
can I KI	cannot K-N	can the K-T	can you KAU
could he KOE	could I KOI	could not KONT	could the KAOT
could you KAOU	did a DAI	did he DHE	did I DI
did not D-N	did the D-T	did you DAU	do I DOI
do not DAON	do the DAOT	do you DOU	does not DUNT
does the DUT	from the FR-T	from you FRAU	had a HAI
had he HE	had I HI	had not H-N	had the H-T
had you HAU	have a VAI	have I VI	have not V-N
have the V-T	have you VAU	has a ZAI	has not Z-N
has the Z-T			

☞ *practice the following:*

I read a book about a man who used to raise snakes for a living.
Why don't you ask him about a loan for the building?

What about the payment that is due tomorrow?
Do you know anything about the wiring in this house?

What about you? Do you want to go or not?
Somebody said something about you, but I didn't believe a word they said.

Where are you going after the football game; do you know yet?
The car sped away after the accident and has not been seen since.

Are you or are you not willing to testify in the murder case?
Are you the one who put the car in the garage last night?

He said that he left before the band started to play.
I knew there was going to be an accident, even before the police did.

Can a defendant be tried twice for the same crime?
Can a person be in two places at the same time?

Can he do the job or not? Please let me know by noon tomorrow.
Can he help you in any way?

Can I be of any assistance in solving the crime?

<u>Can I</u> pick up anything for you on the way to the store?

I <u>cannot</u> even begin to think of any way to explain how this happened.
I <u>cannot</u> see the clock from here; do you know what time it is?

<u>Can the</u> door be left open tonight so that I can get in after midnight?
<u>Can the</u> bank please verify that the check was cashed two weeks ago?

<u>Can you</u> go to the store for me?
<u>Can you</u> answer the question with a verbal response, please?

<u>Could he</u> give you a ride to the airport so that you don't have to call a cab?
<u>Could he</u> tell you what time to be there so you won't be late?

<u>Could I</u> interest you in buying a dozen roses?
<u>Could I</u> tell you the reason that I didn't show up at your party last night?

He <u>could not</u> be there at the start of the show.
Mr. Jones said that he <u>could not</u> afford to buy the meat for his stew.

<u>Could the</u> district attorney please present his case in an orderly fashion?
<u>Could the</u> defendant be present for the arraignment?

<u>Could you</u> make sure that no one else is present when you tell me?
<u>Could you</u> pay me the $200 you owe me by next Tuesday?

<u>Did a</u> strange looking man pass by here about half an hour ago?
<u>Did a</u> pink elephant with purple polka dots do a dance on Main Street?

<u>Did he</u> confess to the murder like he said he was going to?
<u>Did he</u> or did he not tell you that he was there last night at that time?

<u>Did I</u> see what I thought I saw?
<u>Did I</u> tell you about the new car I bought yesterday?

I <u>did not</u> have anything to do with the murder at all.
She <u>did not</u> even ask me if I wanted to go with her to the movie.

<u>Did the</u> insurance man see you about paying your premium on time?
<u>Did the</u> teacher tell you not to bring your dog to class anymore?

<u>Did you</u> appreciate the dinner dance they held in your honor last night?
<u>Did you</u> happen to see the doctor on the way out of the hospital?

<u>Do I</u> have any mustard on my face from the ham sandwich I just ate?
<u>Do I</u> owe you any more money for the trip we took together to Disneyland?

I know that you <u>do not</u> like to put relish on your hamburger.
I <u>do not</u> want to interrupt you, but there is a fire on the back porch.

<u>Do the</u> people who run the supermarket know that they don't have any milk?
<u>Do the</u> trees look funny to you today, or is it my eyes?

<u>Do you</u> want to play a quick game of football before we go to the game?
<u>Do you</u> want me to telephone your mom and tell her you'll be late?

She <u>does not</u> want to have anything to do with you any more.
The guarantee <u>does not</u> cover the cost of shipping and handling for all parts.

<u>Does the</u> answer you just gave coincide with the answer you gave Monday?
<u>Does the</u> cost of the car include air conditioning and a stereo?

He was looking at it <u>from a</u> different perspective than I was.
She comes <u>from a</u> large family; in fact, she has 12 sisters and 3 brothers.

The meter will start <u>from the</u> time you get in the cab until you get out.
I knew he was guilty <u>from the</u> moment I first saw him.

I knew the card was <u>from you</u> even before I opened it up and saw your name.
I don't want anything <u>from you</u>; I can do it myself.

I knew a girl named Mary who <u>had a</u> little lamb.
Did you know that the defendant <u>had a</u> gun that looked just like this one?

<u>Had he</u> not been able to answer the question, I think he would have lied.
<u>Had he</u> been anywhere near the place that caught fire last night?

<u>Had I</u> not seen it for myself, I never would have believed it.
<u>Had I</u> been there, it would have been a completely different story.

I <u>had not</u> even made arrangements for my sister to come visit.
She <u>had not</u> met him; he just assumed that she knew him.

<u>Had the</u> water been turned on yet?
<u>Had the</u> fire department ever had a drill at the school?

<u>Had you</u> ever noticed anything strange about the way he walked?
<u>Had you</u> been receiving these letters in the mail for a long time?

<u>Have I</u> been a pest during my stay in your home?
<u>Have I</u> offended you in any way?

I <u>have not</u> even begun to fight.
I <u>have not</u> yet been able to determine the cause of the fire.

We will <u>have the</u> party at my house starting at 7 o'clock.
John said he did not <u>have the</u> keys to the car.

<u>Have you</u> seen the new hospital they built?
<u>Have you</u> been to the lawyer's office yet to talk about your testimony?

The nurse <u>has a</u> lot of information to fill out on the forms before the surgery.
Art <u>has a</u> problem when it comes to finances; he can't save a penny.

John <u>has not</u> even begun to study for the exam yet.
The new store <u>has not</u> yet had a grand opening.

<u>Has the</u> man from the hardware store called you about your order?
<u>Has the</u> police officer informed you of your rights?

PHRASE DRILL - B

☞ *learn the following*:

he can HAEK	he could HAEKD	he did HAED	he had HAEH
he is HAES	he will HAEW	I can AOIK	I could AOIKD
I did AOID	I had AOIH	I have AOIV	I will AOIW
if he FE	if I FI	if not F-N	if the F-T
if you FAU	in a NAI	in the N-T	into the NAOT
is a SAI	is he SE	is it ST-	is not S-N
is that STHA	is the S-T	is there STR-	is this STHI
it can T-K	it could T-KD	it did T-D	it had T-H
it will T-W	on the OT	or the R-RT	that are THAR
that can THAK	that could THAKD	that did THAD	that had THAH
that have THAV	that he THAE	that is THAS	that the THAT
that you THAU	that will THAW (1)		

(1) The word "thaw" is written THAUW.

☞ *practice the following*:

He can call you on the phone if he wants to; he just doesn't want to.
If he can, he'll be there at 3 o'clock sharp.

He could have been there on time, but he started talking to his friends.
He said he could do it, but now I'm not so sure.

He did have a reason for being late; he broke his leg.
John said he did want to see you again.

He had to go to the doctor because he had an infection.
What he had to do was to drop out of school and get a job.

He is not here; I don't know where he is.
He told me that he is not to be disturbed.

He will walk home with you if you ask him.
Joe said he will help you with your homework tonight.

I can call the police from here.
My mother told me I can go to the store all by myself.

I could ask you to leave right now.
My father told me I could get a new car for my birthday.

83

I did have a friend who lived in New Jersey, but she moved.
When I was working, I did have enough money to buy what I wanted.

I had to be at the airport by noon, but I didn't leave until ten.
Once upon a time, I had a cat and a dog and a goldfish.

I have six brothers and seven sisters in my family.
You know that I have very little money to spare.

I will ask you just one more time.
She said that I will have plenty of time to get my picture taken.

If he will go to the store, ask him to pick up some ice cream.
Did you know that if he got one more strike he would have a perfect game?

If I were you, I wouldn't say anything to him.
If I didn't know you better, I'd say you were not telling the truth.

If you're going, fine; if not, don't.
Answer the question; if not, you'll go to jail.

If the man at the store doesn't have any more, what can you do?
I'll buy the car, if the price is right.

If you want to pass the exam, just study.
If you want to go 225 words a minute, just practice day and night.

I'm in a lot of trouble.
My mother and father are in a new apartment complex.

In the event of an emergency, call for help.
I'm in the middle of watching my favorite television program.

I ran into the man next door at the bank
My brother drove his car into the city last night without permission.

There is a fly in my soup and a bee in my milk.
He is a very difficult person to get along with.

Is he the man you saw at the scene of the crime, or is he not?
When is he going to get there? He's already an hour late.

Is it time to go yet?
Is it okay if I take the car tonight?

This <u>is not</u> the color of paint I asked you to get; I wanted blue. This is green.
Peg <u>is not</u> about to jeopardize her job just because you want a ride home.

<u>Is that</u> the same car that we saw yesterday at the mall?
<u>Is that</u> the defendant sitting at the table with the defense attorney?

<u>Is the</u> color of the car red or orange?
What type of dog <u>is the</u> dog you currently have?

<u>Is there</u> a doctor in the house?
<u>Is there</u> an easier way of getting there or not?

<u>Is this</u> the way you treat a friend?
<u>Is this</u> or is this not the right phone number?

If <u>it can</u> be done, he'll do it.
<u>It can</u> be said that you tried your hardest.

She said <u>it did</u> take a lot of effort on her part, but she didn't mind.
Even though the camera was old, <u>it did</u> take excellent pictures.

My cat was gone for six days; <u>it had</u> kittens.
<u>It had</u> to be wrong; it just didn't fit.

<u>It is</u> time to take the test; are you ready?
<u>It is</u> important to know your limitations before you attempt anything.

The weatherman said that <u>it will</u> rain tomorrow.
<u>It will</u> be difficult for you to find the keys in this mess.

The scratch <u>on the</u> car would not come off.
I placed a large vase <u>on the</u> counter yesterday; now, it is gone.

Is it the first exit <u>or the</u> second exit that we take?
I didn't want to go to the store <u>or the</u> mall.

Do you know how many apples <u>that are</u> rotten?
I saw six cars <u>that are</u> not supposed to be on this side of the road.

Do you know any dogs <u>that can</u> sing?
He told me if <u>that can</u> happen, anything can happen.

<u>That could</u> be the correct answer; you'll have to look it up.
He said that he thinks that <u>that could</u> do it.

The man <u>that did</u> the painting does not live here any more.
He's the one <u>that did</u> it; he's the one that murdered her!

How many people do you know <u>that have</u> two television sets?
Do you know any cars <u>that have</u> four-wheel drive?

He said <u>that he</u> would not leave the building without a hostage.
She said <u>that he</u> was nowhere to be found.

I know <u>that I</u> had a twenty-dollar bill in my wallet, but now I can't find it.
Who said <u>that I</u> have to take the test over again?

<u>That is</u> not the same answer you gave a minute ago.
<u>That is</u> the most ridiculous thing I've ever heard in my life.

He told me <u>that the</u> locks on the garage had all been changed.
I knew <u>that the</u> tire was flat because it was not round.

What is it <u>that you</u> want?
What is it <u>that you</u> do for a living?

<u>That will</u> have to do for now.
Is there anything <u>that will</u> change your mind?

PHRASE DRILL - C

☞ *learn the following*:

there are THR-R	there can THR-K	there could THR-KD	there did THR-D
there had THR-H	there have THR-V	there is THR-S	there will THR-W
they are THER	they can THEK	they could THEKD	they did THED
they had THEH	they have THEV	they will THEW	this is THIS
this will THIW	under the DERT	was a WAI	was he WAE
was I WAOI	was not WAEN	was the WAT	we are WER
we can WEK	we could WEKD	we did WAED (1)	we had WEH
we have WEV	we will WEW	were you WRAU	what a WHAI
what are WHAR	what can WHAK	what could WHAKD	what did WHAD
what had WHAH	what have WHAV	what he WHAE	what I WHAOEU
what is WHAS	what the WHAT	what you WHAU	what will WHAW

(1) The word "wed" is written WED.

☞ *practice the following*:

There are six people waiting to see the doctor this morning.
There are only three who made an appointment.

There can be no doubt about it--he's the one who did it.
There can only be one way of answering the question.

There could be more than one way to do it.
There could be a secret message found in the book.

There did not appear to be anything wrong with the car.
There did seem to be a problem with the generator.

There have been five phone calls for you this morning.
There have been over 20 people looking at the apartment.

There is nothing wrong with your dog.
There is something you can do for me.

There will be a man here tomorrow morning at 11 o'clock.
There will be no excuses given.

They are all going to go to the airport together.
They are not going to make you pay for the damage at this time.

87

They can take their money and spend it on whatever they want.
They can have a choice of pie or cake, but not both.

They could open up the cottage to their friends.
They could offer you a ride to the mall.

They did offer to pay your way to Europe.
They did have an extra cot for you to sleep on.

They had to leave early because one of them got sick.
They had six different people tell them not to go.

They have a wonderful family.
They have to score six more points in order to win the game.

They will not be going to the concert with you tonight.
They will ask you for your opinion.

This is going to be an interesting event.
This is the way to gain speed--practice!

This will help your stomachache.
This will convince you not to drive and drink.

The walkway is under the bridge on the left-hand side of the highway.
Do not miss the small print under the large letters.

There was a snowstorm coming from the mountains.
He did not now that I was a private investigator for the insurance company.

Was he the man who shot you or not?
Was he in the bank at the time of the holdup?

Was I with you the night of the murder?
Was I going to drive you to the supermarket or to the cleaners?

Joe was not aware that he could buy one and get one free.
Penny was not a very good cook; she burned everything.

Was the man from the water department here today?
Was the main reason you did not buy the car because of the color?

We are going to meet you at the corner at noon.
We are all in this together.

We can take a trip to Mexico or Canada.
We can offer you bread and water.

We could bring in the state police to help find the child.
We could take part in the program.

We did offer to baby-sit for your children from 7 until 11.
We did the best we could under the circumstances.

We had to have five more signatures by midnight.
We had forgotten all about the incident.

We have ten more years to go on our mortgage.
We have no more money to give you at this time.

We will offer you free room and board in exchange for your skills.
We will be at the conference on March 17.

Were you there when the bomb exploded?
Were you aware that sixteen people were injured seriously?

Do you know what a short form is?
He wanted to know what a cat was doing in the doghouse.

What are you up to?
What are the chances of your passing the course with a B?

What can I do about it now?
What can you say?

What could have happened to your sister?
What could you give for the cause?

What did he do with the money she gave him?
What did you say?

What had he done?
He wanted to know what had happened to his drink.

What have you to say?
What have you got behind your back?

What he did was to ignore your advice and sell his car.
What he may have done was to go fishing.

<u>What I</u> do and what I say are two different things.
<u>What I</u> want to know is why there are so many fish in the deep blue sea?

<u>What is</u> the meaning of this?
<u>What is</u> the reason for the sky being so pink tonight?

<u>What the</u> man in the truck did was to cut off the car.
Raymond and Sue wanted to know <u>what the</u> sign said before they entered.

Do <u>what you</u> want to do, you always do.
If <u>what you</u> said is true, the game should have started a half hour ago.

<u>What will</u> happen to the children now that the mother is in jail?
<u>What will</u> be will be.

PHRASE DRILL - D

☞ *learn the following*:

when are WH-R	when can WH-K	when could WH-KD	when did WH-D
when had WH-H	when have WH-V	when is WH-S	when the WH-T
when you WHU	when I WHAOI	when will WH-W	where are WHR-R
where can WHR-K	where could WHR-KD	where did WHR-D	where had WH-H
where have WHR-V	where is WHR-S	where the WHR-T	where you WHRAU
where will WHR-W	which are WHIR	which can WHIK	which could WHIKD
which did WHID	which had WHIH	which have WHIV	which is WHIS
which will WHIW	will have L-V	will he LE	will I LI
will not L-NT	will the L-T	will you LAU	with a WAI
would have WOV	would I WOI	would not WOUN	would the WOT
would you WAOU	you are UR	you can UK	you could UKD
you did UD	you had UH	you have UV	you will UW

☞ *practice the following*:

When are you going to shovel the sidewalk?
When are we supposed to arrive at the party; do you know?

When can we see the kittens?
When can you come over to my new house to visit?

When could you be here with the cash?
When could I meet you at the garage?

When did he say he was going to leave?
When did you see him last?

When had you last been there?
When had you ever said anything like that before?

When have I seen you before?
When have we met?

When is the man from the phone company going to get here?
When is there going to be a new moon?

When the man next door called, he said it was an emergency.
When the woman started the car, it began to smoke badly.

When you talk to him next week, ask him if he'll see me.

91

When you type at your computer, do you look at your fingers?

When will he be here?
When will I see you next?

Where are you going to meet him?
Where are you going on vacation next month?

Where can I get a copy of the transcript?
Where can we talk without being interrupted?

Where could he be?
Where could the new book I bought yesterday have gone?

Where did you say you were going to have dinner?
Where did John buy his new computer; do you know?

Where had you been when I called last week?
Where had you gone when I stopped by your house?

Where have all of the flowers gone?
Where have you put the instructions to the printer?

Where is my hat and coat?
Where is my daughter; do you know?

I asked where the men's room was, but no one knew.
I simply wanted to know where the train station was.

I didn't ask you where you were going.
Can you tell me where you got those new gloves?

Where will I ever find a car like the one I had?
Where will you be at 3 o'clock tomorrow afternoon?

Do you mind if I ask you which are going and which are staying?
Which are you? A leader or a follower?

Which can you do?
Computers save time, which can save you money.

Which could be right?
He opened the wrong door, which could be the reason he got lost.

Which did you say you were going to do?
Which did you choose; the red or green one?

I had a computer which had a small hard drive.
I got a new computer which had a larger hard drive.

Which have you chosen? The one on the right or the one on the left?
Which have you picked for your vacation? Florida or California?

Which is easier for you to do? Go to the store now or go to the mall?
Which is the right answer? Yes or no?

Which will you decide to do?
He wanted to know which will he be driving? The Cadillac or the Volkswagen?

We will have six extra people for dinner tonight.
She did not know that we will be out of the country until December 4.

Will I see you before you go to prison?
Will I be able to start a charge account with your department store today?

He said that John will not be able to purchase any more meat at the grocery store.
Diane will not be here until tomorrow.

Will the man in the blue shirt and green tie please stand and approach the bench?
Will the computer be fixed by the time the exams start?

Will you please pass the salt and pepper?
Will you answer the phone for me?

I am going to meet with a lawyer today to discuss the case.
She said she was with a friend last night when the place was robbed.

If I were you, I would have nothing to do with her.
He said he would have six new books for me to pick up.

My question is, would I know you if I saw you?
He asked me, would I like to go to a party at his house.

I would not buy a new car when I could get a good used one.
He said he would not go anywhere without his credit card.

Would you please let me know if I can take the exam today or tomorrow?
Would you forget about what happened last night.

You are the most obstinate person I have ever met.
You are who you are, and that's that.

<u>You can</u> be assured that we will guarantee every product that we have.
<u>You can</u> come along if you want to.

<u>You could</u> go to the zoo while we go to the mall.
I asked if <u>you could</u> get me the Smith file.

<u>You did</u> not hear a word I said.
I would like to know if <u>you did</u> your chores today or not.

<u>You have</u> got to speak louder if you want to be heard by the jury.
<u>You have</u> to pass the exam with a 75 in order to qualify for the position.

<u>You will</u> appreciate all that your mother and father do for you some day.
<u>You will</u> have to ask permission to go in there.

PHRASE DRILL - E

☞ *learn the following:*

I am AOIM	I believe AOIBL	I can AOIK	I could AOIKD
I did AOID	I had AOIH	I have AOIV	I know AOIN
I notice AOINTS	I object AOIB	I recall AOIRL	I recollect AOIRK
I remember AOIRM	I say AOIS	I see AOIZ	I think AOIFK
I understand AOINDZ	I want AOIWT	I was AOIWS	I will AOIW
I would AOIWD			

☞ *practice the following:*

I am not going to ask you to do it one more time.
If you think I am going to pay your way this time, you'd better think again.

If I tell you I believe in you, believe me, I do.
I believe he was trying to get away at the time of the accident.

I can make a pie out of strawberries and crushed graham crackers.
I can probably pass my 225 word per minute speed take today or tomorrow.

I could have had a free ticket to Disneyland, but I lost my lucky numbers.
He said that I could have one kitten from the litter, but I couldn't pick one.

I did have a date for tonight, but he stood me up.
If I did it, then why am I able to not do it now?

I had to take my brother to the dentist yesterday after he broke a tooth.
If I had twenty bucks, I could get the new CD that I want to play for you.

I have no way of knowing what you are thinking; you have to tell me.
John said that I have to concentrate on my studies before the exam.

I know that he didn't do it, but do you know that he didn't?
I know a man who sells seashells by the seashore.

I notice that you're not wearing your raincoat today; why?
I notice that you keep on staring at my new glasses.

I object on the grounds that it is immaterial, irrelevant, and incompetent.
I object because he is not answering the question.

I recall a time, many years ago, when I was in a similar situation.
I recall a woman by the name of Joan who played the harp.

I recollect a date, but I don't know the exact time.
I recollect you had something to do with it, but what I don't know.

I remember you; you're the one who stepped on my toe.
I remember the name of the man; his name was Steve Reeve.

I say, do not call me on the telephone at my home or at my office.
I say no sometimes, and sometimes I say yes; but today, I say maybe.

I see a boat on the water, but I can't make out what kind it is.
I see a car approaching the intersection, and I think it is the one we want.

I think I can do it if I just try.
I think I know the situation.

I understand you to say that you were not present at the time of the crime.
I understand now, thanks to your explanation.

I want you to go with me to the store so that I won't get lost.
I want you to pick me up a loaf of bread and a dozen eggs.

I was led to believe that you were the one who could help me.
I was not able to see the defendant at that time.

I will have to ask you to leave right now, or I'll call the police
I will have a party for you, but you have to tell me when you want it.

I would not go with him because he was a stranger.
I would like to know if you have had anything to eat today.

☞ *learn the following:*

at that time TAMT	at the time TEMT	at this time TIMT
in that case NAS	in the case NES	in this case NIS
if I can FIK	if I could FIKD	if I did FID
if you can FAUK	if you could FAUKD	if you did FAUD

☞ *practice the following:*

Where were you at that time?
What was the position of the automobile at that time?

At the time of the accident, were you driving or were you a passenger?
What was the extent of damage to the truck at the time you saw it?

At this time, we would like to ask everyone who has a phone to leave.
I don't recall at this time whether or not the lady wore a red or a blue dress.

In that case, what do you think about the way she treated you?
In that case, you may leave the witness stand.

In the case of an emergency, please leave the building quickly.
He knew that in the case of extreme temperatures, he would need water.

What is the problem in talking about what took place in this case?
In this case, we have two suspects; one male and one female.

If I can ask you to drive by my mother's house, I would appreciate it.
If I can have a dollar, I'll buy you something.

If I could bother you, may I have a quarter for a cup of coffee?
If I could not do it, I wouldn't have offered.

If I did anything to hurt you, let me know.
If I did the right thing, let me know.

If you can be there by seven, that would be great.
If you can please refrain from whistling while I'm talking, I'd appreciate it.

If you could call an ambulance for me, I would be very thankful.
If you could help me with my homework, I would be grateful.

If you did do it, let us know.
If you did steal the money, you should return it.

☞ *learn the following:*

is that correct STHAK	is that right STHART	is that true STHAT
that is correct THAK	that is right THART	that is true THIT
that's correct THAEK	that's right THAERT	that's true THAET
isn't that correct SNAEK	isn't that right SNAERT	isn't that true SNAET

☞ *practice the following:*

You want eight pieces; is that correct?
He wants to go to the moon; is that correct?

John and Martha are getting engaged; is that right?
The store closes at noon on Sunday; is that right?

There are nine cats in the house; <u>is that true</u>?
Your homework is not done; <u>is that true</u>?

<u>That is correct</u>. He ate the whole cake.
<u>That is correct</u>. Paul ate nine worms.

<u>That is right</u>. The moon is full tonight.
<u>That is right</u>. You can buy six for the price of eight.

<u>That is true</u>. He left about 8 o'clock.
<u>That is true</u>. It snowed 18 inches in one hour yesterday.

<u>That's correct</u>. He confessed to the murder.
<u>That's correct</u>. She will not give you the answers.

<u>That's right</u>. The cow jumped over the moon.
<u>That's right</u>. There are 6,000 people waiting in line.

<u>That's true</u>. The color of the house was pink.
<u>That's true</u>. The printer printed over 600 pages a minute.

☞ *learn the following:*

how far HOUF	how fast HOUSZ	how large HOULG	how late HOULT
how long HOUNG	how many HOUM	how many times HOUMTS	how much HOUCH
how often HOUFN	how old HOULD	how was HOUWZ	how wide HOUWD

☞ *practice the following:*

<u>How far</u> do you have to go to get home?
<u>How far</u> is it from here to Denver?

<u>How fast</u> can your new sports car go?
<u>How fast</u> does the plane fly?

<u>How late</u> are you allowed to stay out at night?
<u>How late</u> do I have to work today?

<u>How long</u> will it be before you will be home?
<u>How long</u> can you endure the pain?

<u>How many</u> women were in the shop during the sale?
<u>How many</u> documents are being introduced into evidence?

How many times have you been arrested?
How many times will you try telephoning her?

How much does the new house cost?
How much money do you have with you?

How often do you do your homework?
How often does he call you?

How old is your mom?
How old was the man who attempted to take your purse?

How was the movie last night?
How was your blind date?

How wide was the doorway?
How wide did you say the truck was?

How large a man was he?
How large was the box that your parents sent you?

PHRASE DRILL - F

☞ *learn the following:*

are not R-N	aren't R-NZ	cannot K-N	can't K-NZ
could not KONT	couldn't KONZ	did not D-N	didn't D-NZ
does not DUNT	doesn't DUNZ	do not DAON	don't DAONZ
had not H-N	hadn't H-NZ	has not Z-N	hasn't Z-NZ
have not V-N	haven't V-NZ	is not S-N	isn't S-NZ
should not SHOUN	shouldn't SHOUNZ	was not WAN	wasn't WANZ
would not WOUN	wouldn't WOUNZ	will not L-NT	won't WOENZ
	aint AINZ	I am AOIM	I'm AOIMZ
they are THER	they're THERZ	you are UR	you're URZ
we are WER	we're WERZ	it will T-W	it'll T-WZ
she will SHAEW	she'll SHAEWZ	we will WEW	we'll WEWZ
he will HAWS	he'll HAEWZ	I will IW	I'll IWZ
how is HOWS	how's HOWZ	that is THAS	that's THAZ
what is WHAZ	what's WHAZ	who is WHOS	who's WHOZ
it is T-S	it's T-Z	there is THR-S	there's THR-Z
where is WHR-S	where's WHR-Z	they have THEV	they've THEFZ
you have UV	you've UVZ	we have WEV	we've WEVZ
I have AOIV	I've AOIVZ	he would HAEWD	he'd HAEDZ
they would THEWD	they'd THEDZ	I would AOIWD	I'd AOIDZ
she would SHAEWD	she'd SHAEDZ	we would WEWD	we'd WAEDZ
you would UWD	you'd UDZ		

☞ *practice the following:*

We <u>are not</u> going to do any shopping today.
We <u>aren't</u> very happy about the outcome of the trial

I <u>cannot</u> condone what you are about to do.
I <u>can't</u> understand why he isn't here today.

I <u>could not</u> help but laugh over his predicament.
I <u>couldn't</u> hear what the bailiff was saying.

I <u>did not</u> want to interrupt you while you were reading.
I <u>didn't</u> go to the circuit when it was in town.

He <u>does not</u> even know why he has to apologize to his sister.
He <u>doesn't</u> have a driver's license or an ID card.

100

We <u>do not</u> have any reason to doubt you.
We <u>don't</u> have an answer to your inquiry.

I <u>had not</u> considered any other alternative.
I <u>hadn't</u> come up with a solution to the problem.

She <u>has not</u> bothered to call home in over a week.
He <u>hasn't</u> attended the meetings since September.

I <u>have not</u> yet begun to fight.
I <u>haven't</u> seen the election results

<u>She is</u> not to go into that store again without her mother's permission.
<u>She's</u> not available to take a deposition today.

You know that you <u>should not</u> pay that much money for a pair of shoes.
You <u>shouldn't</u> have answered the door that night.

John <u>was not</u> guilty.
Amy <u>wasn't</u> aware of her brother's predicament

She <u>would not</u> shovel the sidewalk because she did not feel like it.
He <u>wouldn't</u> answer the phone after 10:00 o'clock.

The principal <u>will not</u> ask you to recite the poem at the assembly.
He <u>won't</u> have an answer to your question until Thursday.

The defendant said he <u>is not</u> the one who did it.
He <u>ain't</u> the one who I identified in the line up.

<u>I am</u> about to enter the twilight zone.
<u>I'm</u> very sorry about the death of your sister.

<u>They are</u> all going to go to Arizona next month.
<u>They're</u> not interested in going skiing this weekend.

<u>You are</u> cordially invited to attend a birthday party at my house.
<u>You're</u> probably one of my best friends.

<u>We are</u> going to wash the car right now.
<u>We're</u> going to register the car with the Department of Motor Vehicles.

<u>It will</u> be at least another six hours before the plane arrives from New York.
<u>It'll</u> be time for you to leave in about an hour.

She will ask you to go to the prom with her.
She'll never see her mother or father again.

We will have to ask the manager for a refund.
We'll have to send the samples to the main factory for inspection.

He will refuse to go with her.
He'll never be able to face her again.

I will show you how to get to the drug store from here.
I'll show you the study books for the state test on Friday.

How is your aunt doing?
How's your uncle doing.

That is the fastest way to get there.
That's the only way to go.

What is your name again?
What's going to happen if he is acquitted.

Who is going to chaperone the party?
Who's going to lend you the books to study with?

It is not for me to say whether or not you can drive there.
It's a problem that we have not been able to solve.

There is nothing left for you to do.
There's absolutely nothing left in the refrigerator to eat.

Where is everybody?
Where's the copy of the World Atlas

They have all gone away.
They've never been to the State of Texas

You have got to do something about your barking dog.
You've always been a good friend of mine.

We have over $16,000 saved up for a new house.
We've never charged more than $20 to the account.

I have had enough to eat for one day.
I've visited several of the sites that you mentioned.

He said <u>he would</u> be home by midnight.
He said <u>he'd</u> never be found guilty.

<u>They would</u> all have to have flu shots at the same time.
<u>They'd</u> all have to attend the concert to get credit in the class.

<u>I would</u> not go in there if I were you.
<u>I'd</u> rather not go to Toronto with you.

<u>She would</u> spend all the money she had if she could.
<u>She'd</u> like to see the coin collection.

<u>We would</u> take a trip around the world if you paid for it.
<u>We'd</u> better register to vote before November 1.

<u>You would</u> have to take a train, a plane, and then a bus to get there.
<u>You'd</u> better make sure you take a raincoat.

PHRASE DRILL - G

☞ Using the KAU as the root for all "can you" phrases, learn the following:

can you KAU	can you believe KAUBL	can you ever KAUFR
can you find KAUFND	can you have KAUV	can you know KAUN
can you notice KAUNTS	can you please KAUP	can you please tell KAUPT
can you please tell us KAUPTS	can you recall KAURL	can you recollect KAURK
can you remember KAURM	can you say KAUS	can you see KAUZ
can you tell KAUT	can you tell us KAUTS	can you think KAUFK
can you understand KAUNDZ		

☞ Now practice the phrases in the following sentences:

Can you enter the race before the January 25 deadline?
Can you pass the potatoes without dropping them on the floor?
Can you mail the letter for me before noon?

Can you believe it is going to rain again tomorrow?
Can you believe that the test is going to be canceled?
Can you believe that Ron and Sue are going to get married?

Can you ever forgive me for not telling you what time the train came in?
Can you ever do your homework on time?
Can you ever reach 110 words per minute?

Can you find the key to success and happiness?
Can you find any bread in the cupboard?
Can you find out what time the train leaves for New Mexico?

Can you have a cat and dog in the house at the same time?
Can you have a party at noon tomorrow, or should we wait until Sunday?
Can you have the office completely redecorated by Monday, September 1?

Can you know the difference between right and wrong?
Can you know the right road to take to get to grandma's house?
Can you know how to spend less money and get more for every dollar?

Can you notice the man in the doorway or not?
Can you notice the color the traffic light?
Can you notice the stop sign behind the tree on the right-hand corner?

Can you please pass the salt and pepper before the food gets cold?
Can you please direct me to the administration building?
Can you please turn off all of the lights when you leave the room?

Can you please tell me the difference between a sapphire and a ruby?
Can you please tell the class what to do in case of an emergency?
Can you please tell Jim when to go and when to stop?

Can you please tell us where to go?
Can you please tell us the best way to get to 250 words a minute?
Can you please tell us when you first saw the lady at the door?

Can you recall the date of the accident?
Can you recall the name of the man who gave you the gun?
Can you recall your birthday?

Can you recollect the facts relating to the fire at all?
Can you recollect the first time you every heard him say the word "snow"?
Can you recollect the last time you dated him?

Can you remember how old you were on your last birthday?
Can you remember the names of all of the people who were at the party?
Can you remember your address at all?

Can you say with a reasonable degree of certainty where you were?
Can you say without any hesitation that you were not there?
Can you say where you were born and what year you were born?

Can you see the sign or not?
Can you see the signature on that piece of paper?
Can you see where the "x's" are located on this drawing?

Can you tell me your age?
Can you tell me your occupation?
Can you tell the District Attorney your reason for being here today?

Can you tell us what you saw on the day of the accident?
Can you tell us what you said to the man who bumped into you?
Can you tell us what you did after you left the apartment house yesterday?

Can you think of any reason why we should not arrest you?
Can you think of an answer to the question or not?
Can you think of an example to help illustrate your point?

Can you understand the question or can't you?
Can you understand Spanish, French, German, and English?
Can you understand the degree of danger you are in at this time?

PHRASE DRILL - H

☞ Using the SPWA as the root for all "I can't" phrases, learn the following:

I can't SPWA	I can't believe SPWABL	I can't ever SPWAFR
I can't find SPWAFND	I can't have SPWAV	I can't know SPWAN
I can't notice SPWANTS	I can't mean SPWAM	I can't mean to SPWAMT
I can't mean to say SPWAMTS	I can't recall SPWARL	I can't recollect SPWARL
I can't remember SPWARM	I can't say SPWAS	I can't see SPWAZ
I can't tell SPWAT	I can't think SPWAFK	I can't understand SPWANDZ

☞ Now practice the phrases in the following sentences:

I can't imagine how he got in here without a key.
I can't give you a ticket to go to the concert unless you give me $100.
I can't tell you the secret because I promised that I would not tell a soul.

I can't believe you did that.
I can't believe my eyes.
I can't believe that you are going to parachute out of an airplane.

I can't ever follow directions.
I can't ever do the right thing.
I can't ever put things in their proper perspective without help.

I can't find the right words to say.
I can't find the needle I lost in the haystack.
I can't find my hat.

I can't have my cake and eat it too.
I can't have another red cent without doing my chores.
I can't have any more fun because I am grounded for three months.

I can't know without your telling me, can I?
I can't know which way to go without a map.
I can't know how much it cost unless I see the price tag.

I can't notice things like that without my glasses on.
I can't notice signs because I just can't.
I can't notice colors like you can because I'm color blind in one eye.

I can't mean it; I really can't.
I can't mean what I say, can I?
I can't mean what I can't mean, unless I really mean it.

I can't mean to do it; I really can't.
I can't mean to tell you what I'm telling you, can I?
I can't mean to do what I do, unless I really mean it.

I can't mean to say the things I say.
I can't mean to say yes if I really mean no.
I can't mean to say one thing and mean to say another thing.

I can't recall if I locked the door or not; can you look for me?
I can't recall what I said yesterday afternoon; can you remind me?
I can't recall the name of the defendant, but I know his sister-in-law.

I can't recollect the address right now.
I can't recollect the color of the car, but I think it was blue and white.
I can't recollect the time I arrived at the scene, but it was around 1 o'clock.

I can't remember right now.
I can't remember what I was supposed to get at the store; I forgot my list.
I can't remember every little detail about the accident; how could I?

I can't say with 100 percent surety.
I can't say yes or no.
I can't say that I am positive, but I will say maybe.

I can't see the house from here; the trees are in the way.
I can't see how you can say something like that without checking the facts.
I can't see anything wrong with that answer, can you?

I can't tell you how much it means to me to have you here.
I can't tell you right now because I really do not know.
I can't tell you if I don't know, can I?

I can't think right now; my mind is a blank.
I can't think of anything to say in response to your question.
I can't think of any reason why he would do such a thing.

I can't understand how you could walk all that way alone.
I can't understand why you would spend all that money for nothing.
I can't understand you; please speak louder if you will.

PHRASE DRILL - I

☞ Using the TPWA as the root for all "I cannot" phrases, learn the following:

I cannot TPWA	I cannot believe TPWABL	I cannot ever TPWAFR
I cannot find TPWAFND	I cannot have TPWAV	I cannot know TPWAN
I cannot notice TPWANTS	I cannot mean TPWAM	I cannot mean to TPWAMT
I cannot mean to say TPWAMTS	I cannot recall TPWARL	I cannot recollect TPWARBG
I cannot remember TPWARM	I cannot say TPWAS	I cannot see TPWAZ
I cannot tell TPWAT	I cannot think TPWAFK	I cannot understand TPWANDZ

☞ Now practice the phrases in the following sentences:

I cannot go with you right now.
I cannot find my coat or my hat anywhere.
I cannot answer the question; I just don't know the answer.

I cannot believe you would say something like that.
I cannot believe that you would do something like that.
I cannot believe that you would go to the store and forget the milk.

I cannot ever imagine the snow coming down that fast.
I cannot ever agree with what you say.
I cannot ever forgive you.

I cannot find the right key.
I cannot find the answer in the book without looking at the index.
I cannot find a car that I like on the entire lot.

I cannot have any ice cream or cookies on my diet.
I cannot have any peace in my house with all that noise.
I cannot have a good relationship with my stepbrother without fighting.

I cannot know which way to go unless you tell me.
I cannot know what answer to give you without looking it up.
I cannot know how old you are without guessing.

I cannot notice anything without my glasses on.
I cannot notice the type of automobile you have unless you tell me.
I cannot notice the book on the table unless I see it.

I cannot mean what I say.
I cannot mean what I do.
I cannot mean how I act.

I cannot mean to do the things I do.
I cannot mean to go where I go.
I cannot mean to cause the trouble I cause.

I cannot meant to say the things I say.
I cannot mean to say what I just said.
I cannot mean to say that at all; you put words into my mouth.

I cannot recall ever having such a more difficult day in my entire life.
I cannot recall of ever having heard anyone say something like that before.
I cannot recall at this time.

I cannot recollect the color, the car, or the make or year.
I cannot recollect the address of the defendant, but I know it was on Main.
I cannot recollect his name, but I think it started with a "J" or a "G".

I cannot remember, and that's the truth.
I cannot remember what he said to me right now; I just cannot remember.
I cannot remember anything.

I cannot say with absolute certainty at this time.
I cannot say that it was he or not.
I cannot say yes or no.

I cannot see the forest for the trees.
I cannot see how you can say something like that in front of the jury.
I cannot see how you can do something like that.

I cannot tell from this angle what the shape of the box was.
I cannot tell you right now because I honestly do not remember a thing.
I cannot tell where the one line ends and the other line begins.

I cannot think right now; I have too much on my mind.
I cannot think of a good answer.
I cannot think of any reason why he should not be found guilty.

PHRASE DRILL - J

☞ Using the KAOU as the root for all "could you" phrases, learn the following:

could you KAOU	could you believe KAOUBL	could you ever KAOUFR
could you find KAOUFND	could you have KAOUV	could you know KAOUN
could you notice KAOUNTS	could you please KAOUP	could you please tell KAOUPT
could you please tell us KAOUPTS	could you recall KAOURL	could you recollect KAOURK
could you remember KAOURM	could you say KAOUS	could you see KAOUZ
could you tell KAOUT	could you tell us KAOUTS	could you think KAOUFK
could you understand KAOUNDZ		

☞ Now practice the phrases in the following sentences:

<u>Could you</u> pass the salt and pepper?
<u>Could you</u> identify the defendant as the woman you saw at the scene?

<u>Could you believe</u> the story that he was telling you?
<u>Could you believe</u> him or not?

<u>Could you ever</u> imagine that such a thing would happen?
<u>Could you ever</u> go to the school again after what happened yesterday?

<u>Could you find</u> the paper you were looking for?
<u>Could you find</u> the words to say or not?

<u>Could you have</u> had anything to do with the murder?
<u>Could you have</u> been mistaken when you identified the defendant?

<u>Could you know</u> what you were doing in such a state of mind?
<u>Could you know</u> it was going to happen?

<u>Could you notice</u> anything in particular about the way he was dressed?
<u>Could you notice</u> the name on the side of the truck from where you were?

<u>Could you please</u> mention what time you arrived at the restaurant?
<u>Could you please</u> ask the person sitting next to you to stop talking?

<u>Could you please tell</u> me your name and address for the record?
<u>Could you please tell</u> his Honor what time you left the store?

<u>Could you please tell us</u> what you were doing there that day at that time?
<u>Could you please tell us</u> your answer without getting carried away?

110

Could you recall for me the time you left the police station?
Could you recall the names of any other individuals who helped you?

Could you recollect the day of the week it happened?
Could you recollect the month of the year it happened?

Could you remember the name of the town you were in last night?
Could you remember the man and woman who asked you for the money?

Could you say whether or not you were intoxicated at that time?
Could you say whether or not you were under the influence of any drugs?

Could you tell me your purpose in going there that evening?
Could you tell Mr. Jones why you didn't go home the regular way?

Could you tell us what your answer is right now, please?
Could you tell us if you are going to go to the hospital or stay home?

Could you think that such a thing could happen?
Could you think of any answer other than the one you gave?

Could you understand the question or not?
Could you understand why I had to do what I had to do?

PHRASE DRILL - K

☞ Using the SPWU as the root for all "I couldn't" phrases, learn the following:

I couldn't SPWU	I couldn't believe SPWUBL	I couldn't ever SPWUFR
I couldn't find SPWUFND	I couldn't have SPWUV	I couldn't know SPWUN
I couldn't notice SPWUNTS	I couldn't mean SPWUM	I couldn't mean to SPWUMT
I couldn't mean to say SPWUMTS	I couldn't recall SPWURL	I couldn't recollect SPWURK
I couldn't remember SPWURM	I couldn't say SPWUS	I couldn't see SPWUZ
I couldn't tell SPWUT	I couldn't think SPWUFK	I couldn't understand SPWUNDZ

☞ Now practice the phrases in the following sentences:

I couldn't eat another bite.
I couldn't answer the question because I didn't know how.

I couldn't believe that he said such a thing about me.
I couldn't believe what I saw.

I couldn't ever do such a thing.
I couldn't ever commit such a crime.

I couldn't find my wallet or my license when the policeman asked for them.
I couldn't find my way out of the tunnel; I was lost.

I couldn't have been there because I have an alibi.
I couldn't have telephoned you because I was out of the country.

I couldn't know what he said; I couldn't hear a thing.
I couldn't know which way to go; I'm lost.

I couldn't notice the sign because you were standing in front of it.
I couldn't notice the temperature.

I couldn't mean what I said; please forgive me.
I couldn't mean it; I just couldn't.

I couldn't mean to do what I just did.
I couldn't mean to make you do it either.

I couldn't mean to say what I just said.
I couldn't mean to say what you think I just said.

I couldn't recall the date of the anniversary.
I couldn't recall the name of the ship that he sailed on.

I couldn't recollect how many people were in the bus at the time.
I couldn't recollect whether it was raining or snowing at that time.

I couldn't remember what I told him.
I couldn't remember what time I was supposed to meet the plane.

I couldn't say yes, and I couldn't say no.
I couldn't say maybe, either.

I couldn't see the forest for the trees.
I couldn't see the sign behind the building, could I?

I couldn't tell you whether I did or did not; I can't remember.
I couldn't tell you if I was there or not.

I couldn't think of anything to say.
I couldn't think of any reason why I was supposed to go.

I couldn't understand the reason he gave me for smashing my car.
I couldn't understand why he had to go out when his brother was home.

PHRASE DRILL - L

☞ Using the TPWU as the root for all "I could not" phrases, learn the following:

I could not TPWU	I could not believe TPWUBL
I could not ever TPWUFR	I could not find TPWUFND
I could not have TPWUV	I could not know TPWUN
I could not noitce TPWUNTS	I could not mean TPWUM
I could not mean to TPWUMT	I could not mean to say TPWUMTS
I could not recall TPWURL	I could not recollect TPWURK
I could not remember TPWURM	I could not say TPWUS
I could not see TPWUZ	I could not tell TPWUT
I could not think TPWUFK	I could not understand TPWUNDZ

☞ Now practice the phrases in the following sentences:

I could not count backwards from 100 to 1.
I could not even count the number of fingers on my hands.

I could not believe that the plane crashed and that no one heard it.
I could not believe that the snow was so deep that it covered the roof.

I could not ever do something like that.
I could not ever ask for a refund after I wore the dress to a party.

I could not find the jacket that I left at the banquet.
I could not find my keys to the car so I had to call a taxi.

I could not have said that.
I could not have told you that.

I could not know which way to turn; I was intoxicated at the time.
I could not know how much the computer cost; I didn't ask the salesman.

I could not notice the tag on the computer; it was covered up.
I could not notice the dog hiding behind the door.

I could not mean what I said.
I could not mean for you to walk all the way home without a ride.

I could not mean to do that; I just could not.
I could not mean to have you arrested; I just wanted to warn you.

I could not mean to say that; you know me better than that.
I could not mean to say, yes, when I really meant to say, no.

I could not recall why you told me you were here; please tell me again.
I could not recall the year or make of the automobile.

I could not recollect my age when the announcer asked me.
I could not recollect my name after I got hit on the head with the bat.

I could not remember a thing that happened to me before the accident.
I could not remember why I went to the store.

I could not say how the accident happened.
I could not say one way or the other.

I could not see from where I was standing.
I could not see the parade, so I moved to a better spot.

I could not tell you because I was too upset at the time.
I could not tell him the number of times I had been by there before.

I could not think of any reason why he could not come over to visit me.
I could not think of a sentence to write, so I made one up.

I could not understand why he had to pressure me into going with him.
I could not understand the formula he used to explain the theory.

PHRASE DRILL - M

☞ Using the DAU as the root for all "did you" phrases, learn the following:

did you TAU	did you believe DAUBL	did you ever DAUFR
did you find DAUFND	did you have DAUV	did you know DAUN
did you notice DAUNTS	did you mean DAUM	did you mean to DAUMT
did you mean to say DAUMTS	did you recall DAURL	did you recollect DAURK
did you remember DAURM	did you say DAUS	dd you see DAUZ
did you tell DAUT	did you tell us DAUTS	did you think DAUFK
did you understand DAUNDZ		

☞ Now practice the phrases in the following sentences:

<u>Did you</u> do anything to wake the cat?
<u>Did you</u> walk, run, or jog to the office this morning?

<u>Did you believe</u> that statement the defendant made yesterday?
<u>Did you believe</u> her story?

<u>Did you ever</u> walk in the evening moonlight?
<u>Did you ever</u> talk to the police officer about the accident?

<u>Did you find</u> anybody home at all?
<u>Did you find</u> his story believable?

<u>Did you have</u> anything to do with the murder?
<u>Did you have</u> a party here last night?

<u>Did you know</u> the defendant before the crime?
<u>Did you know</u> him at all?

<u>Did you notice</u> anything about his appearance at all?
<u>Did you notice</u> the way he looked at you?

<u>Did you mean</u> what you just said?
<u>Did you mean</u> that he was here or not here when you said that?

<u>Did you mean to</u> do it or not?
<u>Did you mean to</u> go left or right at the corner?

<u>Did you mean to say</u> what you just said?
<u>Did you mean to say</u> you saw seven or seventeen people?

Did you recall that at that time?
Did you recall going there before the accident?

Did you recollect talking to the defendant at any time?
Did you recollect the name of the man you bought the car from?

Did you remember seeing her as she stepped off the curb?
Did you remember a fight between the plaintiff and the defendant?

Did you say you would do it or not?
Did you say anything to her at all?

Did you see him or not?
Did you see the accident happen?

Did you tell me you were on the stand for direct examination?
Did you tell the Court that you were involved in this crime or not?

Did you tell us a little while ago that you paid $500 for the computer?
Did you tell us that you lost your credit card and then you found it?

Did you think that you could get away with the crime?
Did you think that your actions were warranted?

Did you understand the question?
Did you understand anything your attorney asked you at all?

PHRASE DRILL - N

☞ Using the SPWEU as the root for all "I didn't" phrases, learn the following:

I didn't SPWI	I didn't believe SPWIBL	I didn't ever SPWIFR
I didn't find SPWIFND	I didn't have SPWIV	I didn't know SPWIN
I didn't notice SPWINTS	I didn't mean SPWIM	I didn't mean to SPWIMT
I didn't mean to say SPWIMTS	I didn't recall SPWIRL	I didn't reccollect SPWIRK
I didn't remember SPWIRM	I didn't say SPWIS	I didn't see SPWIZ
I didn't tell SPWIT	I didn't think SPWIFK	I didn't understand SPWINDZ

☞ Now practice the phrases in the following sentences:

I didn't want anything to do with her at all.
I didn't hear what you said; please repeat the question.

I didn't believe a word he said.
I didn't believe her for one minute.

I didn't ever do that.
I didn't ever go in that store on the day in question.

I didn't find the key, so I had to break the window.
I didn't find any truth in your answers.

I didn't have anything to do with the murder, and you know it.
I didn't have a quarter to phone home.

I didn't know you were going to be at the party.
I didn't know what to say, so I said nothing.

I didn't notice you behind the tree.
I didn't notice anything about his physical features at all.

I didn't mean what I said.
I didn't mean that you were supposed to leave.

I didn't mean to do it.
I didn't mean to have you ask him for a date with me.

I didn't mean to say that.
I didn't mean to say what I said.

I didn't recall anything about the night before.
I didn't recall your calling me on the phone.

I didn't recollect the name of the person who waited on me.
I didn't recollect the license plate number.

I didn't remember the question.
I didn't remember your asking me that.

I didn't say that.
I didn't say you could go in there without me.

I didn't see you at the graduation ceremony.
I didn't see you in church last Sunday.

I didn't tell you you could do that.
I didn't tell you to write a letter to him.

I didn't think you were serious.
I didn't think that the other plaintiff was going to press charges.

I didn't understand your question at all.
I didn't understand why he was there that morning.

PHRASE DRILL - O

☞ Using the TPWEU as the root for all "I did not" phrases, learn the following:

I did not TPWI	I did not believe TPWIBL
I did not ever TPWIFR	I did not find TPWIFND
I did not have TPWIV	I did not know TPWIN
I did not notice TPWINTS	I did not mean TPWIM
I did not mean to TPWIMT	I did not mean to say TPWIMTS
I did not recall TPWIRL	I did not recollect TWPIRK
I did not remember TPWIRM	I did not say TPWIS
I did not see TPWIZ	I did not tell TPWIT
I did not think TPWIFK	I did not understand TPWINDZ

☞ Now practice the phrases in the following sentences:

I did not want to go in there alone.
I did not hear you.

I did not believe a word he said.
I did not believe her story at all.

I did not ever say that to her on that date.
I did not ever go in the store and make that purchase.

I did not find the blouse I was looking for.
I did not find the keys to the car.

I did not have the foggiest idea.
I did not have any intention of suing her.

I did not know which way to go.
I did not know how to do it.

I did not notice anything unusual that night.
I did not notice that there were three people in there.

I did not mean what I said.
I did not mean for you to get so angry.

I did not mean to crash the car.
I did not mean to flunk the test.

I did not mean to say Pontiac; I meant to say Cadillac.
I did not mean to say for her to leave the store.

I did not recall why I went there.
I did not recall the Social Security number he told me.

I did not recollect anything.
I did not recollect the make of the truck.

I did not remember what I had for supper last night.
I did not remember anything on the test at all.

I did not say, yes; I said, no.
I did not say anything to you.

I did not tell him where to go.
I did not tell her anything at all about where I was that evening.

I did not think I could stop in time.
I did not think I could pass the test.

I did not understand why he wanted me to pay him so much money.
I did not understand where he was coming from.

PHRASE DRILL - P

☞ Using the DAOU as the root for all "do you" phrases, learn the following:

do you DOU (1)	do you believe DAOUBL
do you ever DAOUFR	do you find DAOUFND
do you have DAOUV	do you know DAOUN
do you notice DAOUNTS	do you mean DAOUM
do you mean to DAOUMT	do you mean to say DAOUMTS
do you recall DAOURL	do you recollect DAOURK
do you remember DAOURM	do you say DAOUS
do you see DAOUZ	do you tell DAOUT
do you tell us DAOUTS	do you think DAOUFK
do you understand DAOUNDZ	

(1) While the phrase "do you" is written DOU, the DAOU is used as the root for all phrases.

☞ Now practice the phrases in the following sentences:

Do you want to go out to dinner tonight or order something?
Do you appreciate the things that your friend does for you?

Do you believe in reincarnation?
Do you believe that he committed the crime?

Do you ever get lost when you're out driving around?
Do you ever wish you could grow money on a tree?

Do you find that if you ignore the problem the problem will go away?
Do you find it true that most people are friendly?

Do you have anything to add?
Do you have any questions?

Do you know anyone who will watch my dog for the weekend?
Do you know anyone who wants to buy a house?

Do you notice anything different about me?
Do you notice that sign above your head?

Do you mean that I can't go with you?
Do you mean I'm not invited to the party?

122

Do you mean to drive down this one-way street?
Do you mean to turn right at the corner?

Do you mean to say that you ate that whole pie by yourself?
Do you mean to say there's nothing left in the cupboard?

Do you recall visiting your sick aunt on the night of the murder?
Do you recall where you were?

Do you recollect saying that you would fix the water heater?
Do you recollect where you were going at the time?

Do you remember anything about the man you saw?
Do you remember what kind of a truck it was?

Do you say yes, or do you say no?
Do you say that you now can't remember?

Do you see me?
Do you see the signature at the bottom of the document?

Do you tell people what to do and where to go?
Do you tell lies all the time or just when you're under oath?

Do you tell us the truth when you are on the stand?
Do you tell us anything different today?

Do you think you are smart?
Do you think he committed the murder or not?

Do you understand the question?
Do you understand what I mean?

PHRASE DRILL - Q

☞ Using the SPWO as the root for all "I don't" phrases, learn the following:

I don't SPWO	I don't believe SPWOBL
I don't ever SPWOFR	I don't find SPWOFND
I don't have SPWOV	I don't know SPWON
I don't notice SPWONTS	I don't mean SPWOM
I don't mean to SPWOMT	I don't mean to say SPWOMTS
I don't recall SPWROL	I don't recollect SPWORK
I don't remember SPWORM	I don't say SPWOS
I don't see SPWOZ	I don't tell SPWOT
I don't think SPWOFK	I don't understand SPWONDZ

☞ Now practice the phrases in the following sentences:

I don't read books; I watch television.
I don't like to ride in an airplane if I can drive.

I don't believe you.
I don't believe I have had the pleasure of meeting you before.

I don't ever want to hear you say those words again.
I don't ever want to go in that house again.

I don't find any evidence that he was here.
I don't find the answer anywhere in the book.

I don't have anything to say.
I don't have any money to buy a ticket.

I don't know if I can do it or not.
I don't know what time she said to meet her at the market.

I don't notice anything new about your appearance.
I don't notice the smell; do you?

I don't mean it, I really don't.
I don't mean what I say.

I don't mean to cause any trouble.
I don't mean to hurt anyone.

I don't mean to say anything wrong.
I don't mean to say what I say when I say it, it just comes out that way.

I don't recall anyone asking you to come along.
I don't recall my inviting you.

I don't recollect having said that at any time.
I don't recollect your name right now.

I don't remember anything about this place.
I don't remember my name or address since the accident.

I don't say things like that.
I don't say yes when I mean no. ·

I don't see anything wrong with your going out tonight.
I don't see where you are coming from.

I don't tell people what to do, unless they ask.
I don't tell lies.

I don't think you know what I mean.
I don't think I can explain it any better.

I don't understand what she means.
I don't understand the instruction booklet at all.

PHRASE DRILL - R

☞ Using the TPWO as the root for all "I do not" phrases, learn the following:

I do not TPWO	I do not believe TPWOBL
I do not ever TPWOFR	I do not find TPWOFND
I do not have TPWOV	I do not know TPWON
I do not notice TPWONTS	I do not mean TPWOM
I do not meant to TPWOMT	I do not mean to say TPWOMTS
I do not recall TPWORL	I do not recollect TPWORK
I do not remember TPWORM	I do not say TPWOS
I do not see TPWOZ	I do not tell TPWOT
I do not think TPWOFK	I do not understand TPWONDZ

☞ Now practice the phrases in the following sentences:

I do not collect the taxes in this department.
I do not appraise property as a living, just as a hobby.

I do not believe you can eat all of that in one hour.
I do not believe your answers.

I do not ever want to see you in this building again.
I do not ever want to hear you say those words again.

I do not find anything wrong with his credibility.
I do not find any plausible alibi.

I do not have any reason that I can think of to doubt his credibility.
I do not have the correct change at this moment.

I do not know the answer.
I do not know how or why he could have committed the murder.

I do not notice things like that.
I do not notice anything wrong with the way he walks or talks.

I do not mean the greenhouse; I mean the green building.
I do not mean it was snowing at that particular time.

I do not mean to go anyplace where I am not supposed to go.
I do not mean to justify his actions at all.

I do not mean to say anything I am not supposed to say.
I do not mean to say he can go with you.

I do not recall his asking permission to be here.
I do not recall his signing his name on the proper line.

I do not recollect his having been so angry before.
I do not recollect the weather conditions at this time.

I do not remember your name.
I do not remember where you said you were from.

I do not say one way or the other.
I do not say at this time; I do not know.

I do not see you; please turn on a light.
I do not see what you mean; please explain further.

I do not tell lies when I am asked direct questions.
I do not tell people off, only when I'm upset.

I do not think you should be here.
I do not think you can do it.

I do not understand why you came here in the first place.
I do not understand why you would not pay your bills on time.

PHRASE DRILL - S

☞ Using the FAU as the root for all "if you" phrases, learn the following:

if you FAU	if you believe FAUBL
if you ever FAUFR	if you find FAUFND
if you had FAUH	if you have FAUV
if you know FAUN	if you notice FAUNTS
if you mean FAUM	if you mean to FAUMT
if you mean to say FAUMTS	if you please FAUP
if you recall FAURL	if you recollect FAURK
if you remember FAURM	if you say FAUS
if you see FAUZ	if you tell FAUT
if you tell us FAUTS	if you think FAUFK
if you understand FAUNDZ	

☞ Now practice the phrases in the following sentences:

If you want to go to the store with me, you better hurry.
If you need to have some money, just let me know.

If you believe that he committed the murder, please tell someone.
If you believe that you are doing the right thing, then do it.

If you ever come across a 1942 Indian head copper penny, let me know.
If you ever go to China, pick me up a hat.

If you find out who did it, let me know.
If you find my keys, please give me a call.

If you had it to do over again, would you?
If you had more money, you could probably buy the car you want.

If you have to go, you have to tell the supervisor.
If you have too many eggs in your basket, you'll drop them.

If you know the perpetrator, tell me.
If you know how I can make some money, will you please let me know?

If you notice anything wrong while I'm away, call the police.
If you notice a strange looking man hanging around the house, that's my dad.

If you mean what you say, then say what you mean.
If you mean June rather than July, then you are correct.

128

If you mean to offer the exhibit in evidence, please say so.
If you mean to make me angry, you have succeeded.

If you mean to say something, you may not.
If you mean to say that he was the one responsible, please speak up.

If you recall the date of the accident, please tell us.
If you recall where you were yesterday at noon, let us know.

If you recollect the name of the song, you should let someone know.
If you recollect the make of the car, write it down.

If you remember where you bought your bag, I'd like to buy one.
If you remember anything at all, you'd better begin to answer my questions.

If you say he did it, then he did it.
If you say you saw him, then one of you must be lying.

If you see me, don't say anything.
If you see the man in this courtroom, point him out.

If you tell stories, let me hear one.
If you tell me where you hid the money, I won't tell anyone.

If you tell us what you did with the murder weapon, we'll go easy on you.
If you tell us where you were last night, you'll have an alibi.

If you think that I'm going to put on that hat, you've got another thing coming.
If you think that you can call him know, you'd better think twice.

If you understand, please nod your head.
If you understand the reason for his being so disruptive, let me know.

PHRASE DRILL - T

☞ Using the LAU as the root for all "will you" phrases, learn the following:

will you LAU	will you believe LAUBL
will you ever LAUFR	will you find LAUFND
will you have LAUV	will you know LARN
will you notice LAUNTS	will you mean LAUM
will you mean to LAUMT	will you mean to say LAUMTS
will you please LAUP	will you please tell LAUPT
will you please tell us LAUPTS	will you recall LAURL
will you recollect LAURK	will you remember LAURM
will you say LAUS	will you see LAUZ
will you tell LAUT	will you tell us LAUTS
will you think LAUFK	will you understand LAUNDZ

☞ Now practice the phrases in the following sentences:

Will you pass the liver and onions?
Will you leave me alone so I can get my work done?

Will you believe me if I show you?
Will you believe me if I provide an eyewitness?

Will you ever get over your cold?
Will you ever have enough money?

Will you find the answer to peace and happiness?
Will you find out why the dog has been barking all night?

Will you have one more glass of milk before you go?
Will you have to get up early in the morning?

Will you know it when you see it?
Will you know me by my voice?

Will you notice the new sign on the outside of the building?
Will you notice what I say and when I say it?

Will you mean it?
Will you mean the left or the right when you signal me?

Will you mean to have him arrested?
Will you mean to limit the amount of money she can have in the settlement?

Will you mean to say that?
Will you mean to say something different when you speak?

Will you please let us know when you plan on arriving?
Will you please pass the ketchup?

Will you please tell me what you said to him?
Will you please tell me what you think of my new pink hat?

Will you please tell us when he comes through the doorway?
Will you please tell us the reason for your leaving so soon?

Will you recall anything at all?
Will you recall his name and address?

Will you recollect what date he died?
Will you recollect his age?

Will you remember where you were born?
Will you remember to bring home a loaf of bread?

Will you say what time you want to eat?
Will you say where he came from?

Will you see me to the door?
Will you see if I can order a subscription, also?

Will you tell the judge where you were?
Will you tell your lawyer what it is you want to say?

Will you tell us how old you are?
Will you tell us your present occupation?

Will you think of a good answer while I stall him?
Will you think about it for the next two weeks or so?

Will you understand if I explain it to you differently?
Will you understand where I'm coming from if I go into detail?

PHRASE DRILL - U

☞ Using the SPWOE as the root for all "I won't" phrases, learn the following:

I won't SPWOE	I won't believe SPWOEBL
I won't ever SPWOEFR	I won't find SPWOEFND
I won't have SPWOEV	I won't know SPWOEN
I won't notice SPWOENTS	I won't mean SPWOEM
I won't mean to SPWOEMT	I won't mean to say SPWOEMTS
I won't recall SPWOERL	I won't reccollect SPWOERK
I won't remember SPWOERM	I won't say SPWOES
I won't see SPWOEZ	I won't tell SPWOET
I won't think SPWOEFK	I won't understand SPWOENDZ

☞ Now practice the phrases in the following sentences:

I won't go with you.
I won't eat supper tonight; I'm going out on a date.

I won't believe it until I see it.
I won't believe a word you say.

I won't ever do it again, I promise.
I won't ever tell you another secret as long as I live.

I won't find out; how could I?
I won't find anything wrong, I'm sure.

I won't have anything to do with the dog in the house.
I won't have you say things like that.

I won't know what to do if I did do it.
I won't know who he is, since I never met the man before in my life.

I won't notice anything, I promise.
I won't notice you at the dance without your green tuxedo.

I won't mean it when I say it.
I won't mean it, I promise.

I won't mean to do anything to hurt you.
I won't mean to open the chips; I can't help it.

I won't mean to say anything.
I won't mean to say it.

I won't recall a thing; I just know I won't.
I won't recall your name after you leave.

I won't recollect where you came from without help.
I won't recollect anything for the exam.

I won't remember where you said you were born.
I won't remember a thing about what happened yesterday.

I won't say a word.
I won't say yes or no.

I won't see you after tomorrow.
I won't see him anymore; he left town on the train.

I won't tell you what I think.
I won't tell a sole about where we've been.

I won't think about it anymore.
I won't think anything less of you if you tell me where you got it.

I won't understand until you do tell me.
I won't understand a thing unless he explains it better.

PHRASE DRILL - V

☞ Using the WAOU as the root for all "would you" phrases, learn the following:

would you WAOU	would you believe WAOUBL
would you ever WAOUFR	would you find WAOUFND
would you have WAOUV	would you know WAOUN
would you notice WAOUNTS	would you mean WAOUM
would you mean to WAOUMT	would you mean to say WAOUMTS
would you recall WAOURL	would you recollect WAOURK
would you remember WAOURM	would you say WAOUS
would you see WAOUZ	would you tell WAOUT
would you tell us WAOUTS	would you think WAOUFK
would you understand WAOUNDZ	

☞ Now practice the phrases in the following sentences:

Would you ask the man in front of you to remove his hat?
Would you pass the popcorn?

Would you believe I forgot my wallet?
Would you believe me if I told you I was an alien from outer space?

Would you ever consider asking him for a date?
Would you ever testify in court against him?

Would you find a way home if I were to leave now?
Would you find a solution to the problem?

Would you have anything to offer?
Would you have to telephone home if I told you it was after midnight?

Would you know which way to turn at the intersection?
Would you know how many pieces of gold are missing?

Would you notice anything different about the car if I showed you this photograph?
Would you notice the time he comes in the door and let me know?

Would you mean by that that you just don't know?
Would you mean your mother or father when you say your parent?

Would you mean to do that?
Would you mean to knock him out if you hit him?

Would you mean to say that?
Would you mean to say all those things you said about him?

Would you recall any event at all that may have been noteworthy?
Would you recall for us the time of departure?

Would you recollect your whereabouts the night of the murder?
Would you recollect where you parked your car if I drove you around the lot?

Would you remember to call me by ten o'clock?
Would you remember to shut the door and lock it when you leave?

Would you say he was tall or short?
Would you say that he did not suffer any injuries as a result of the accident?

Would you see if he can come out and play?
Would you see if he can testify tomorrow?

Would you tell your mother that I don't need to borrow the money after all.
Would you tell your father that I need to borrow $50?

Would you tell us the temperature the night of the accident?
Would you tell us how old you are at the present time?

Would you think that he could have done it?
Would you think of any reason at all for the way he acted?

Would you understand my questions better if you sat up here?
Would you understand him a little more if he were to explain things?

☞ Using the SPWOU as the root for all "I wouldn't" phrases, learn the following:

I wouldn't SPWOU	I wouldn't believe SPWOUBL
I wouldn't ever SPWOUFR	I wouldn't find SPWOUFND
I wouldn't have SPWOUV	I wouldn't know SPWOUN
I wouldn't notice SPWOUNTS	I wouldn't mean SPWOUM
I wouldn't mean to SPWOUMT	I wouldn't mean to say SPWOUMTS
I wouldn't recall SPWOURL	I wouldn't recollect SPWOURK
I wouldn't remember SPWOURM	I wouldn't say SPWOUS
I wouldn't see SPWOUZ	I wouldn't tell SPWOUT
I wouldn't think SPWOUFK	I wouldn't understand SPWOUNDZ

☞ Now practice the phrases in the following sentences:

I wouldn't go in there if I were you.
I wouldn't call him on the phone at this time of night.

I wouldn't believe a word he says.
I wouldn't believe you if you swore in open court.

I wouldn't ever hurt a flea.
I wouldn't ever lie to you.

I wouldn't find my way out of a paper bag.
I wouldn't find anything wrong with him if I were you.

I wouldn't have anything to do with her.
I wouldn't have a party on Friday the 13th.

I wouldn't know whom to call in case of emergency.
I wouldn't know what to do.

I wouldn't notice his tie if I were you.
I wouldn't notice anything about his hair.

I wouldn't mean it, I promise.
I wouldn't mean it if I said it; you know that.

I wouldn't mean to call you a name.
I wouldn't mean to ask you a personal question like that.

I wouldn't mean to say anything like that.
I wouldn't mean to say blue when I meant red.

I wouldn't recall anything after two years.
I wouldn't recall his name.

I wouldn't recollect where he came from.
I wouldn't recollect the color of the house.

I wouldn't remember the number on the house, but I do remember the street.
I wouldn't remember what time it happened, but I know it was dark out.

I wouldn't say yes, and I wouldn't say no.
I wouldn't say anything to anybody if I were you.

I wouldn't see anything wrong with that.
I wouldn't see Harry tonight if I were you.

I wouldn't tell you a lie.
I wouldn't tell you anything.

I wouldn't think he would ever do anything like that.
I wouldn't think it was possible, would you?

I wouldn't understand it if I saw it.
I wouldn't understand how he could ever do something like that.

PHRASE DRILL - X

☞ Using the TPWOU as the root for all "I would not" phrases, learn the following:

I would not TPWOU	I would not believe TWOUBL
I would not ever TPWOUFR	I would not find TPWOUFND
I would not have TPWOUV	I would not know TPWOUN
I would not notice TPWOUNTS	I would not mean TPWOUM
I would not mean to TPWOUMT	I would not meant to say TPWOUMTS
I would not recall TPWOURL	I would not recollect TPWOURK
I would not remember TPWOURM	I would not say TPWOUS
I would not see TPWOUZ	I would not tell TPWOUT
I would not think TPWOUFK	I would not understand TPWOUNDZ

☞ Now practice the phrases in the following sentences:

I would not dare to cross the bridge at all.
I would not ask him to do that.

I would not believe his story.
I would not believe a word he says.

I would not ever cross the street alone.
I would not ever tell a lie.

I would not find fault with anyone.
I would not find anything wrong with him.

I would not have anything to do with him anymore.
I would not have to go to the doctor if I didn't catch the flu.

I would not know which way to go without your help.
I would not know how to do my math without you.

I would not notice the white cat in the snow unless it moved.
I would not notice how he did it unless he told me.

I would not mean anything by it.
I would not mean something I didn't mean.

I would not mean to call you on the phone unless I wanted to.
I would not mean to write that letter unless I wanted to.

I would not mean to say that, except I was angry.
I would not mean to say left when I meant to say right.

I would not recall anything without your help.
I would not recall the answers on the exam without someone telling me.

I would not recollect anyone's name at all unless they told me.
I would not recollect how to do it unless I read the instructions again.

I would not remember to go to the store unless I was reminded.
I would not remember to pick you up unless you called me before I left.

I would not say that you were right or that you were wrong.
I would not say anything to Carmen about the accident.

I would not see any better with sunglasses on.
I would not see him to the door because he insulted me.

I would not tell him who did it.
I would not tell the police where I was that night.

I would not think that a crime like that would be committed in this neighborhood.
I would not think that the price of gas would ever be so high.

I would not understand it if it were explained to me in simple English.
I would not understand French or Spanish, but I would understand Italian.

Suggested Answers to Beginning Exercises from Drill I

fan (short a)	ran (short a)	rain (long a)	sign (long i)	ten (short e)	teen (long e)
temp (short e)	boat (long o)	light (long i)	sight (long i)	pure (long u)	muse (long u)
heat (long e)	soap (long o)	drape (long a)	dap (short a)	fright (long i)	fit (short i)
site (long i)	sit (short i)	dope (long o)	dip (short i)	send (short e)	mend (short e)
store (short o)	bore (short o)	rap (short a)	rape (long a)	hit (short i)	owe (long o)
pen (short e)	been (short e)	bean (long e)	lit (short i)	stock (short o)	tow (long o)

5 examples of words that contain the long a:

pain	vain	cane	strain	drain

5 examples of words that contain the long e:

seek	feel	weak	deer	breeze

5 examples of words that contain the long i:

might	pie	site	white	tie

5 examples of words that contain the long o:

soak	vote	row	load	zone

5 examples of words that contain the long u:

cute	lute	cure	sure	pure

5 different examples of prefixes for words:

trans-	under-	down-	ex-	anti-

5 different examples of suffixes for words:

-ment	-action	-mission	-less	-full

5 examples of one syllable words:

two	men	cat	house	snow

5 examples of two syllable words:

fifty	argue	rainy	denture	glasses

5 examples of words containing three or more syllables:

figuratively	momentary	reliable	definitely	wonderful

about a BAEU	could you KAOU
about the B-T	could you believe KAOUBL
about you BAU	could you ever KAOUFR
after the AFRT	could you find KAOUFND
ain't AINZ	could you have KAOUV
are not R-N	could you know KAOUN
are you RAU	could you notice KAOUNTS
aren't R-NZ	could you please KAOUP
at that time TAMT	could you please tell KAOUPT
at the time TEMT	could you please tell us KAOUPTS
at this time TIMT	could you recall KAOURL
	could you recollect KAOURK
before the BFRT	could you remember KAOURM
	could you say KAOUS
can a KAEU	could you see KAOUZ
can he KE	could you tell KAOUT
can I KEU	could you tell us KAOUTS
can the K-T	could you think KAOUFK
can you KAU	could you understand KAOUNDZ
can you believe KAUBL	couldn't KONZ
can you ever KAUFR	
can you find KAUFND	did a DAEU
can you have KAUV	did he DHE
can you KAU	did I DEU
can you know KAUN	did not D-N
can you notice KAUNTS	did the D-T
can you please KAUP	did you DAU
can you please tell KAUPT	did you DAU
can you please tell us KAUPTS	did you believe DAUBL
can you recall KAURL	did you ever DAUFR
can you recollect KAURK	did you find DAUFND
can you remember KAURM	did you have DAUV
can you say KAUS	did you know DAUN
can you see KAUZ	did you mean DAUM
can you tell KAUT	did you mean to DAUMT
can you tell us KAUTS	did you mean to say DAUMTS
can you think KAUFK	did you notice DAUNTS
can you understand KAUNDZ	did you recall DAURL
cannot K-N	did you recollect DAURK
can't K-NZ	did you remember DAURM
could he KOE	did you say DAUS
could I KOEU	did you see DAUZ
could not KONT	did you tell DAUT
could not KONT	did you tell us DAUTS
could the KAOT	did you think DAUFK

did you understand DAUNDZ
didn't D-NZ
do I DOEU
do not DAON
do the DAOT
do you DOU
do you believe DAOUBL
do you ever DAOUFR
do you find DAOUFND
do you have DAOUV
do you know DAOUN
do you mean DAOUM
do you mean to DAOUMT
do you mean to say DAOUMTS
do you notice DAOUNTS
do you recall DAOURL
do you recollect DAOURK
do you remember DAOURM
do you say DAOUS
do you see DAOUZ
do you tell DAOUT
do you tell us DAOUTS
do you think DAOUFK
do you understand DAOUNDZ
does not DUNT
does the DUT
doesn't DUNZ
don't DAONZ

from the FR-T
from you FRAU

had a HAEU
had he HE
had I HEU
had not H-N
had the H-T
had you HAU
hadn't H-NZ
has a ZAEU
has not Z-N
has the Z-T
hasn't Z-NZ
have a VAEU
have I VEU

have not V-N
have the V-T
have you VAU
haven't V-NZ
he can HAEK
he could HAEKD
he did HAED
he had HAEH
he is HAES
he will HAEFRP
he will HAEW
he would HAEWD
he'd HAEDZ
he'll HAEWZ
how far HOUF
how fast HOUSZ
how is HOWS
how large HOULG
how late HOULT
how long HOUNG
how many HOUM
how many times HOUMTS
how much HOUCH
how often HOUFN
how old HOULD
how was HOUWZ
how wide HOUWD
how's HOWZ

I am AOIM
I believe AOIBL
I can AOIK
I cannot believe TPWABL
I cannot ever TPWAFR
I cannot find TPWAFND
I cannot have TPWAV
I cannot know TPWAN
I cannot mean TPWAM
I cannot mean to say TPWAMTS
I cannot mean to TPWAMT
I cannot notice TPWANTS
I cannot recall TPWARL
I cannot recollect TPWARBG
I cannot remember TPWARM
I cannot say TPWAS

I didn't recollect SPWIRBG
I didn't remember SPWIRM
I didn't say SPWIS
I didn't see SPWIZ
I didn't tell SPWIT
I didn't think SPWIFK
I didn't understand SPWINDZ
I do not TPWO
I do not believe TPWOBL
I do not ever TPWOFR
I do not find TPWOFND
I do not have TPWOV
I do not know TPWON
I do not mean TPWOM
I do not mean to say TPWOMTS
I do not mean to TPWOMT
I do not notice TPWONTS
I do not recall TPWORL
I do not recollect TPWORBG
I do not remember TPWORM
I do not say TPWOS
I do not see TPWOZ
I do not tell TPWOT
I do not think TPWOFK
I do not understand TPWONDZ
I don't SPWO
I don't believe SPWOBL
I don't ever SPWOFR
I don't find SPWOFND
I don't have SPWOV
I don't know SPWON
I don't mean SPWOM
I don't mean to say SPWOMTS
I don't mean to SPWOMT
I don't notice SPWONTS
I don't recall SPWORL
I don't recollect SPWORBG
I don't remember SPWORM
I don't say SPWOS
I don't see SPWOZ
I don't tell SPWOT
I don't think SPWOFK
I don't understand SPWONDZ
I had AOIH
I have AOIV

I know AOIN
I notice AOINTS
I object AOIB
I recall AOIRL
I recollect AOIRK
I remember AOIRM
I say AOIS
I see AOIZ
I think AOIFK
I understand AOINDZ
I want AOIWT
I was AOIWS
I will AOIW
I would AOIWD
I would not TPWOU
I would not believe TPWOUBL
I would not ever TPWOUFR
I would not find TPWOUFND
I would not have TPWOUV
I would not know TPWOUN
I would not mean TPWOUM
I would not mean to TPWOUMT
I would not mean to say TPWOUMTS
I would not notice TPWOUNTS
I would not recall TPWOURL
I would not recollect TPWOURBG
I would not remember TPWOURM
I would not say TPWOUS
I would not see TPWOUZ
I would not tell TPWOUT
I would not think TPWOUFK
I would not understand TPWOUNDZ
I wouldn't SPWOU
I wouldn't believe SPWOUBL
I wouldn't ever SPWOUFR
I wouldn't find SPWOUFND
I wouldn't have SPWOUV
I wouldn't know SPWOUN
I wouldn't mean SPWOUM
I wouldn't mean to say SPWOUMTS
I wouldn't mean to SPWOUMT
I wouldn't notice SPWOUNTS
I wouldn't recall SPWOURL
I wouldn't recollect SPWOURBG
I wouldn't remember SPWOURM

I wouldn't say SPWOUS	is a SAI
I wouldn't see SPWOUZ	is he SE
I wouldn't tell SPWOUT	is it ST-
I wouldn't think SPWOUFK	is not S-N
I wouldn't understand SPWOUNDZ	is that STHA
I'd AOEUDZ	is that correct STHAK
if he FE	is that right STHART
if I FI	is that true STHAT
if I can FIK	is the S-T
if I could FIKD	is there STHR-
if I did FID	is this STHI
if not F-N	isn't S-NZ
if the F-T	it can T-K
if you FAU	it could T-KD
if you believe FAUBL	it did T-D
if you can FAUK	it had T-H
if you could FAUKD	it is T-S
if you did FAUD	it will T-W
if you ever FAUFR	it'll T-WZ
if you find FAUFND	it's T-Z
if you had FAUH	I've AOIVZ
if you have FAUV	
if you know FAUN	on the OT
if you mean FAUM	or the R-RT
if you mean to FAUMT	
if you mean to say FAUMTS	she will SHAEW
if you notice FAUNTS	she would SHAEWD
if you please FAUP	she'd SHAEDZ
if you recall FAURL	she'll SHAEWZ
if you recollect FAURK	should not SHOUN
if you remember FAURM	shouldn't SHOUNZ
if you say FAUS	
if you see FAUZ	that are THAR
if you tell FAUT	that can THAK
if you tell us FAUTS	that could THAKD
if you think FAUFK	that did THAD
if you understand FAUNDZ	that had THAH
I'll AOIWZ	that have THAV
I'm AOIMZ	that he THAE
in a NAI	that is THAS
in that case NAS	that is correct THAK
in the N-T	that is right THART
in the case NES	that is true THIT
in this case NIS	that the THAT
into the NAOT	that will THAW

that you THAU
that's THAZ
that's correct THAEK
that's right THAERT
that's true THAET
there are THR-R
there can THR-K
there could THR-KD
there did THR-D
there had THR-H
there have THR-V
there is THR-S
there will THR-W
there's THR-Z
they are THER
they can THEK
they could THEKD
they did THED
they had THEH
they have THEV
they will THEW
they would THEWD
they'd THEDZ
ther're THERZ
they've THEFZ
this is THIS
this will THIW

under the DERT

was he WAE
was I WAOI
was not WAENT
was the WAT
wasn't WAENZ
we are WER
we can WEK
we could WEKD
we did WAED
we had WEH
we have WEV
we will WEW
we would WEWD
we'd WAEDZ
we'll WEWZ

we're WERZ
were you WRAU
we've WEVZ
what are WHAR
what can WHAK
what could WHAKD
what did WHAD
what had WHAH
what have WHAV
what he WHAE
what I WHAOI
what is WHAS
what the WHAT
what will WHAW
what you WHAU
what's WHAZ
where is WHR-S
where's WHR-Z
who is WHOS
who's WHOZ
will not L-NT
will you LAU
will you believe LAUBL
will you ever LAUFR
will you find LAUFND
will you have LAUV
will you know LAUN
will you mean LAUM
will you mean to LAUMT
will you mean to say LAUMTS
will you notice LAUNTS
will you please LAUP
will you please tell LAUPT
will you please tell us LAUPTS
will you recall LAURL
will you recollect LAURK
will you remember LAURM
will you say LAUS
will you see LAUZ
will you tell LAUT
will you tell us LAUTS
will you think LAUFK
will you understand LAUNDZ
won't WOENZ
would not WOUN

would you   WAOU
would you believe WAOUBL
would you ever WAOUFR
would you find WAOUFND
would you have WAOUV
would you know WAOUN
would you mean WAOUM
would you mean to WAOUMT
would you mean to say WAOUMTS
would you notice WAOUNTS
would you recall WAOURL
would you recollect WAOURK
would you remember WAOURM
would you say WAOUS
would you see WAOUZ
would you tell WAOUT
would you tell us WAOUTS
would you think WAOUFK
would you understand WAOUNDZ
wouldn't WOUNZ

you are UR
you have UV
you would UWD
you'd UDZ
you're URZ
you've UVZ